Pelargoniums for all Purposes

During the past decade the genus *Pelargonium* has in this country and else-where staged an astonishing return to popularity. Grown in British gardens since the first half of the seventeenth century, pelargoniums reached a peak of popularity during Queen Victoria's reign, which did not abate until the First World War prohibited the cultivation of these plants in greenhouses. From that time until John E. Cross published his *The Book of The Geranium* in 1951 (the first specialist book on the subject to be published for over 100 years) and articles started to appear in the popular gardening press, interest in the genus languished. In the following year the Geranium Society (now the British Pelargonium and Geranium Society) was formed, and the merits of this flower, in its many forms, have been recognised by an ever-increasing company of gardeners.

As an enthusiast who for many years grew a large collection of pelar-goniums in Essex, and as a founder member of the Geranium Society, in which he has held the offices of Secretary, Editor, Vice-Chairman and Vice-President, Mr Cross is particularly well qualified to write this book on all aspects of pelargonium cultivation. His chapters on the historical aspects of the genus and modern classification, his detailed list of species and varieties and his advice on growing pelargoniums under glass and in the open give the reader a balanced picture of a group of ornamental plants which have much charm and seem likely to win acclaim from an even wider public.

Also by John E. Cross

THE BOOK OF THE GERANIUM

*To Henry J. Wood of the
British Pelargonium and Geranium
Society whose enthusiasm and
encouragement has made this
book possible*

Pelargoniums for all Purposes

JOHN E. CROSS

W. H. & L. COLLINGRIDGE LTD

COVENT GARDEN, LONDON

Published in 1965
by W. H. & L. Collingridge Ltd.
Printed by
Billing & Sons Ltd., Guildford and London

———◆———

Contents

Illustrations

Illustrations

ACKNOWLEDGEMENTS

I would like to thank Mr H. F. Parrott of Cobham, Kent, and Mr. K
McCreadie and Mr E. Hickman of the Southend Parks Department
for their valuable help in providing facilities for taking many of the
photographs reproduced in this book.   *J. E. C.*

CHAPTER ONE

Historical Background

The genus *Pelargonium* is part of the *Geraniaceae*. This is a large family, and its distinguishing feature botanically is the long beak-shaped fruit. The family name is of Greek origin and means, literally, cranesbill.

The genus *Geranium* is part of that family together with the *Pelargonium*. The word geranium is derived from the same Greek word as the family name, but pelargonium comes from a word meaning storksbill. The true geraniums are native plants of this country and Europe and are often cultivated in gardens. They are, in general, completely hardy.

Over many years, by popular usage, the name geranium has also come to be applied to the genus pelargonium. There is indeed some confusion in this matter. As pelargoniums belong to the geranium family, they have some claim to being called geraniums, although in a strictly botanical sense they ought to be called pelargoniums. The experts can argue, but the man in the street will go on calling the 'good old scarlet geranium' by that name, although it is strictly a zonal pelargonium.

The pelargonium is an African plant, and was first discovered by the Dutch in Cape Colony in the opening years of the seventeenth century. By the 1650s many species were being cultivated in Europe. It was not a hardy plant, and required the protection of the first hothouses in the great mansions.

The pelargonium in its natural habitat is a plant of the arid semi-desert of southern Africa. Apart from a few desert species from Australia, and a few single species from Madagascar, St Helena and Tristan da Cunha, all the members of this numerous and intensely varied genus are African in origin.

The pelargonium has been naturalised very successfully on the Mediterranean coasts of Europe and North Africa, and especially in the southern states of America. In California it is practically regarded as a weed. Wherever it grows out of doors, it must have a frost-free climate.

Its astonishing variety of leaf and form are part of the evolutionary processes which protect the plant from drought and the attentions of browsing animals. There are species with spines like a cactus, with tap-roots and swollen stems, and with leaf shapes varying from hair-like ferns to thick, felted plates. The leaves may give off a variety of volatile oils which are reminiscent of peppermint, turpentine, citrus peel, rose petals, and a selection of pungent unidentifiable smells. These are successful in deterring browsing animals such as antelope or goats.

In the hothouses of the plant collectors, the pelargonium species were found to hybridise freely, and so the most famous 'geranium' of all, the single zonal pelargonium with its brilliant red flower and fleshy, zoned leaf, was born. It is probably a cross between *P. inquinans*, the cosmetic geranium (its red petals were used at one time to give a touch of rouge to the cheeks), and *P. zonale*, which has insignificant flowers but a faintly zoned leaf. By 1863, Victor Lemoine had introduced the first double zonal pelargonium, and from this time the popularity of this plant seemed to gain momentum.

The first published accounts of the pelargonium appeared in 1732 in the description of the gardens in Eltham, Kent, of Dr Sherard. By 1802 Andrews had published his famous *Monograph of the Genus Geranium* with its hand-coloured plates. The most famous book on the subject was to follow in 1820, the *Geraniaceae* of Robert Sweet. This was published in five volumes with handsome coloured plates. It established the 'geranium' as a fashionable plant. There is no sign, however, in this erudite work, of the great developments that were soon to follow.

The popularity of the pelargonium soared to its climax during the reign of Queen Victoria and persisted until the 1914-18 war prohibited its cultivation under glass. Between the wars it languished and it was not until the publication of *The Book of the Geranium* in 1951 that articles began to appear in the popular gardening press. Derek Clifford's *Pelargoniums, Including the Popular Geranium*, 1958, is a scholarly work which has done much to clear up the tangle of nomenclature. Two popular books have been published in America: *Geraniums, Pelargoniums for Windows and Gardens*, 1946, by Helen

Van Pelt Wilson, and *Geraniums for Home and Garden*, by Helen K. Krauss, 1955.

The Geranium Society was formed in London during 1952 by a group of enthusiasts. In the autumn of 1964 it was renamed The British Pelargonium and Geranium Society. There had been older specialist societies, but no records remained. Soon after the advent of the new British society, an American society was initiated and the Geranium Society itself aquired affiliated societies in Australia, New Zealand and South Africa. The British Pelargonium and Geranium Society publishes quarterly bulletins of popular interest, and a year-book which contains much valuable material.

Since its introduction into Europe, the pelargonium has always attracted the attention of the plant collectors and hobbyists. Trade nurserymen were quick to take advantage of such an easily propagated plant. Robert Sweet himself was associated with Colville and Co. in supplying the species and hybrids he had publicised in his book. The French nurserymen such as Victor Lemoine of Nancy, and Bruant of Poitiers, were responsible for the introduction of hundreds of new varieties from the 1840s until the early 1900s.

In England, Cannell of Swanley in Kent was breeding and sending out many new kinds. His *Floral Guide* for 1910 lists 800 new and well-tried zonal and regal pelargoniums, many of his own raising.

One of the greatest of the pelargonium enthusiasts in this country was William Alvared Rae Clifton of Chichester. Growing these plants before the First World War, he managed to retain a stock through the fuel restrictions of 1914–18. From 1918 until 1939 he was the only trade specialist. Basing his lists on the older catalogues and especially Cannell's, he kept his stocks true to name, and regularly supplied first-class plants for sixty years. He died in 1962 and will be missed by pelargonium lovers everywhere. His name is associated with many new introductions, including the ivy-leaved variety Mrs W. A. R. Clifton.

From 1950 until the present day, many nurserymen have taken up the pelargonium, and there are a dozen who grow a wide range of varieties and supply high quality plants. Every year many worthy new cultivars are offered to the public, and with the encouragement of The British Pelargonium and Geranium Society these wonderful introductions are shown at the Royal Horticultural Society's shows and regularly win awards.

The pelargonium enthusiast today is offered a bewildering number of varieties. Brilliant new regal pelargoniums from America and many fascinating introductions among the miniature varieties are listed by nurserymen and many of the old and forgotten species and varieties have been rediscovered and given a new lease of life.

Among modern enthusiasts and hybridisers, the tendency is to specialise in one group of this versatile and sizeable family. For instance, Anthony C. Ayton has bred a number of new regal varieties and has been largely instrumental in introducing the much improved new American varieties. One of the most outstanding of these was Grand Slam, raised by William E. Schmidt of Palo Alto, California, who has been responsible for introducing many new varieties. Another famous American geranium specialist is Holmes Miller in Los Altos. He raised many new zonals but has a strong claim to fame for his coloured-leaved miniatures.

H. F. Parrett has specialised in miniatures and zonals with coloured leaves and large flower trusses. R. J. W. Mitchell has pioneered the introduction of new varieties from Switzerland and Czechoslovakia, and Derek P. Clifford has been associated mainly with species, having built up a unique collection of rare pelargoniums.

A suitable
shoot with
two to three
joints

Slicing
the stem
horizon-
tally just
below the
joint

Trimming the cut end

Removing the lower leaves

The stipules are
cut off cleanly . . .

. . . also the flower
buds with
their stems

Making a hole with a dibber

Firming in the
cutting with the
fingers

A full pot, with five
cuttings set around the
edge

CHAPTER TWO

Modern Pelargonium Classification

When the Geranium Society (now the British Pelargonium and Geranium Society) embarked on the preparation of a register of cultivars and species in 1956, the nomenclature sub-committee in the first instance had to face the task of finalising the classification of these plants. This sub-committee was expertly advised by Mr J. S. L. Gilmour, M.A., V.M.H. This classification has now been generally accepted and consists of the following sections: *a*, Zonal pelargoniums; *b*, Regal pelargoniums; *c*, Ivy-leaved pelargoniums; *d*, Hybrid ivy-leaved pelargoniums; *e*, Scented-leaved pelargoniums; *f*, Unique pelargoniums; *g*, Angel pelargoniums, Appendix: *h*, Species; *j*, Primary hybrids.

These alphabetical groups were then expanded as follows:

ZONAL PELARGONIUMS (*Pelargonium* × *hortorum* Bailey)

(*Note:* The leaves of this section do not necessarily have a zonal mark.)

(1) Mature plants normally more than 8 in. high grown principally for their flowers and with petals not twisting into a quill.

(*a*) **Single-flowered Group**, having normally not more than five petals. i, White; ii, Pink; iii, Red; iv, Salmon; v, Orange; vi, Magenta and vii, Picotee and fancy. An excellent example of i is Queen of the Whites, an old variety dating from 1884 and still widely grown. The form of these single zonals is often very pure and symmetrical, and the size of the individual florets in a variety such as Pride of the West can be very large.

The picotee and fancy varieties can be as remarkable as Lady Warwick whose white petals are finely and sharply edged with

magenta, or Mr Wren, an American introduction which has bands of bright scarlet on a white background.

(*b*) **Double and Semi-double-flowered Group.** This has flowers normally composed of six or more petals but not 'hearted' like a rosebud. i, White; ii, Pink; iii, Red; iv, Salmon; v, Orange; vi, Magenta and vii, Picotee and fancy.

The most famous variety in this section is undoubtedly Gustav Emich, the Buckingham Palace geranium. This splendid red flower is now used extensively in public places. It was listed by Cannell in 1898 but it is not likely to be the same plant. Its name and origin are shrouded in mystery. Twenty years ago it was discovered by one of the gardeners of the Royal Parks who begged a few cuttings from a friend at Goodwood. In a few years a large stock had been built up, and it can be seen everywhere nowadays.

The cultivars in this section were mainly developed in France during the latter part of the last century, and many have French names. The flowers are long lasting and do not fall as easily as those in the single-flowered group; this makes them particularly suitable for bedding out.

(*c*) **Rosebud Group.** Fully double and 'hearted', the middle petals remaining unopened like a rosebud. This small group contains a few very choice geraniums whose origins have been lost completely. The best known variety is Red Rambler. The older geranium enthusiasts used to wear a single floret of this variety in their buttonhole in order to mystify the rosarians.

(**2**) Mature plants more than 8 in. high and grown for their flowers, having petals twisted into a quill.

(*d*) **Cactus-flowered Group,** single and double.
One of these 'Poinsettia-flowered' geraniums was known before 1900. This was Fire Dragon, but we have no record as to how it was developed. Some new varieties have come from Schmidt in America, and there are now examples in most of the colour sections.

(**3**) Mature plants normally more than 8 in. high grown principally for their foliage, single and double-flowered.

(*e*) **Fancy-leaved Group.** i, Silver-leaved; ii, Silver tricolors; iii, Golden-leaved; iv, Bronze and gold-leaved; v, Black-leaved (leaves black, purple-black or dark zoned); vi, Butterfly-leaved

(with butterfly markings of distinct tone or hue in centre of leaf); and vii, Golden tricolors.

The great collecting fervour for fancy-leaved geraniums dates from the 1850s when more than 30 examples of silver-leaved geraniums were listed. Mrs Cox, or more correctly Mr Henry Cox, is undoubtedly the best known in this section today. It is a golden tricolor with particularly brilliant leaf markings.

The bronze and gold-leaved section have mainly gold or light green leaves with prominent zones varying from light chestnut to brown. One of the most popular varieties is Maréchal MacMahon, who was President of the Third Republic of France in 1873, as the Duc de Magenta. The plant has a leaf heavily zoned in reddish-brown with small, single, vermilion flowers. The black-leaved section contains but one example, the unusual Distinction. This was listed by Henderson in 1870 and has very dark green leaves with a distinct finer dark zone close to the outer margins.

The next section is the butterfly-leaved, of which the most famous kind is Happy Thought. This was listed by Grieve before 1868 and has a dark green leaf with a distinct yellow and ivory butterfly mark in the centre. The single flowers can be obtained in pink or red forms.

The last section contains the most extraordinary leaf colours of all, and a bed of Mr Henry Cox is a magnificent sight.

(4) Mature plants normally less than 8 in. high, single and double-flowered.

(f) **Miniature Group.** i, Green-leaved; ii, Black-leaved; iii, Silver-leaved and iv, Tricolor.

All the miniature pelargoniums are becoming very popular. One of the best known of the older sorts is Grannie Hewitt, which is a perfect dwarf variety with tiny double flowers. The popular Golden Harry Hieover was known in 1880 but its origins have been lost. Black-leaved types are very common in this group, the best known of which are Red Black Vesuvius and Salmon Black Vesuvius.

REGAL PELARGONIUMS (*Pelargonium × domesticum* Bailey)

(5) Arranged according to principal colour impression of flower. i, White; ii, Pink; iii, Red; iv, Salmon; v, Orange; vi, Magenta and vii, Black.

19

The ancestry of regal pelargoniums is a very confused one and it must be assumed that the species *P. cucullatum*, *P. fulgidum*, *P. reniforme* and *P. grandiflorum* have all contributed to it. The flowers of regals are much larger on the whole than those of zonals and have the form of an azalea. The colour range is larger and there are tones and feather markings of the petals which are not to be found in any other kind of pelargonium. They are mainly grown in greenhouses as pot plants. Nearly three hundred varieties are offered by nurserymen today. Great strides have been made in the United States of America in improving the colour and form of the flowers. Whereas zonals tend to have a twelve-month season of blooming, regals are at their peak during the early part of the summer, when the plants are covered in bloom. The name 'regal' was first used by Cannell in 1877. In America they are called Martha Washingtons and in Germany Edelpelargonien.

In recent years many regals have been given awards by the Royal Horticultural Society, especially Carisbrooke, which received an award of merit in 1952; Grand Slam A.M. 1956, and a First Class Certificate, 1961; and Grandma Fischer (Grossmama Fischer) A.M. 1960. Lord Bute is an older variety with flowers of a purple so dark that it is almost black, edged with carmine.

IVY-LEAVED PELARGONIUMS

(a) Single-flowered, of which the flowers have normally five petals.
(b) Double-flowered, of which the form is fundamentally that of the single-flowered, but the petals normally exceed five.
(c) Rosette, having smaller flowers with more than five petals, more or less equal in size and altering the shape of the flower.

The ivy-leaved pelargoniums all appear to have a common ancestor in *P. peltatum*, so called from the shield-like appearance of its leaf. This shape of leaf, with or without zones, persists in all the modern cultivars. The flowers vary in size, and one of the largest varieties is Leopard, which has a lilac-pink flower with lilac blotches. Another popular and distinctive variety is L'Elégante, which has variegated green and white foliage, and which turns purple under conditions of drought or cold. It is a very floriferous plant and often bears more than a hundred trusses of its pale lilac, single flowers. It received a first-class certificate from the R.H.S. in 1872. Schmidt of California has raised several new varieties of ivy-leaved pelargoniums. It is interesting to note that the scent of the foliage of these plants is reminiscent of crushed ivy leaves.

HYBRID IVY-LEAVED PELARGONIUMS

Although all the ivy-leaved pelargoniums are crosses between *P. peltatum* and other species and sub-species, a special group has been formed where the ancestry is obviously seen to include the zonal hybrids. These ivy×zonal hybrids are unusual plants with leaves similar to zonals and flowers more in character with the ivy section. One of the best of these is Millfield Gem, with large double flowers of pale pink feathered with rose-red.

SCENTED-LEAVED PELARGONIUMS

There are many scented-leaved species, but this section deals mainly with the cultivars. The volatile oils given off by the leaves have a surprisingly wide scent range. Included are the scents of rose, lemon, orange, citron, nutmeg, peppermint, lemon balm, pine, spice, eucalyptus, citronella, apple, camphor, apricot, ginger, and many other pungent smells.

Some nurserymen specialise in these varieties, and they have an old-world attraction for many collectors. One of the best varieties is Clorinda, which has large purple flowers with heavily indented leaves, and a scent reminiscent of both rose petals and eucalyptus.

A very popular variety is Crispum Variegatum, with small curled leaves variegated in cream and green. This variety has a pronounced lemon scent. This plant can be trained into a large fastigiate shrub several feet high. It has been known for more than a hundred years.

UNIQUE PELARGONIUMS

This section was popular nearly one hundred years ago. The outstanding colour impression of the flowers is a very brilliant red, which has been obtained from the species *P. fulgidum*. They are more like regals than any other type of pelargonium, but the leaves are often more irregular and finely divided. Some of them have pungent or scented leaves. The flowers are never as large as the best of the regals, and the colour range is limited. The form of the flowers resembles that of the more primitive of the regals. One of the most famous of these is Crimson Unique.

ANGEL PELARGONIUMS

This section are rather like miniature regals, but they merit a group to themselves. There are about nine varieties available and they were all raised by Arthur Langley Smith. Mr Langley Smith died in April, 1953. He was a schoolmaster in Catford, and a great pelargonium expert and hybridiser. His great success was with the miniatures. The most popular variety of his raising is Catford Belle, which has rose-purple flowers.

SPECIES

The plants int his section are normally those which may be found in a wild state. Over 300 species have been described botanically, but a large number must in point of fact be duplicates.

The scientific description of pelargonium is further complicated by the existence of natural hybrids. As I have already remarked, Derek Clifford in his book on the subject has done much to clarify this nomenclature tangle.

Some species are offered by nurserymen and are well worth growing. One of the most venerable of these is *P. triste*, the 'sad geranium', introduced by Tradescant in 1632. It grows wild in Cape Province. It has carrot-like leaves and small yellow and brown flowers, which are sweetly scented at night. Another species with night-scented flowers is the curious *P. gibbosum* (the gouty geranium) which has long stems, with odd swellings in the joints. Both these species are pollinated by night-flying moths, and it is a strange fact that the scent is only emitted at night.

Pelargonium echinatum, the 'spiny geranium', is also known in America as the 'Cactus geranium' because the plant often sheds its leaves and the bare stems have sharp spines. It was introduced in 1789, and was illustrated by Robert Sweet. The flowers are remarkable, being white splashed with crimson.

Mr H. Hall of the National Botanic Gardens, Kirstenbosch, South Africa, has described how many of these species are often to be found in the wild. I quote his description of *P. echinatum:* 'It is fairly widely distributed in Namaqualand, found on the more shaded hill slopes, frequently straggling under or intermingled with other shrubs—often the brilliant flowers are the only clue to indicate that the Prickly Geranium is near. For when out of flower, their stems and leaves merge quietly into the rest of the shrubs and plants.' The species will continue to be grown by enthusiasts who hope to raise new hybrids and to add even more variety to the pelargonium family.

PRIMARY HYBRIDS

Within this group are placed varieties in cultivation which are natural hybrids. The best known is *P.* × *fragrans*, a short bushy plant whose leaves have a spicy scent. Another is the well-known *P.* × *kewense*. This has dark crimson flowers with narrow petals and is a very free-flowering, bushy plant.

CHAPTER THREE

Planting Out of Doors

It was Charles Dickens who noted that the streets of Victorian London were decorated by the popular geranium. This plant has indeed suffered from the vicissitudes of fashion. In the seventeenth and eighteenth centuries, it was a rare exotic importation, carefully nurtured in hothouses. In the Victorian period it became a vulgar popular bedder, used in parks and the new suburban villa gardens. It was used as a window plant, and bought for a few pence every spring by the populace. This enthusiasm continued until the First World War, when glasshouses were used for food production and tender ornamental plants were consigned, by law, to the compost heap.

The vogue for 'natural gardening' and for labour-saving management spelt the doom of carpet-bedding, and between the wars this worthy plant languished.

The geranium survived in the municipal parks because there was no substitute. Today, the wheel has come full circle, and modern architectural settings demand banks of solid colour. Even under the most adverse of polluted atmospheres the geranium will give of its best.

Formal bedding. It is, of course, a summer-bedding plant. Hundreds of thousands of geranium plants are raised every year for public use. From the beginning of May the geraniums are always in flower, and, provided the dead flower heads are removed, they continue to look neat and colourful.

In their natural habitat in Africa, or in their adopted California, they are in bloom the whole year round, except when periods of drought give them a rest. Conditions in this country are far more difficult, and the plants must not be bedded out until all danger of frost has passed. In addition, there is far too much rainfall and not enough sun to suit them ideally.

Cuttings ready
for potting on

Rooted and
unrooted cuttings

Potting rooted
cuttings

Firming in

A potted cutting

Plants from
cuttings; some
are already
beginning to
flower

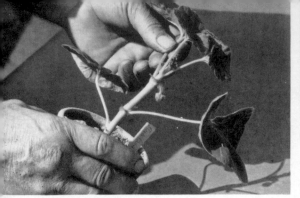

PINCHING OUT

Above left: A young plant ready for pinching out

Above right: The growing tip is removed, and the flower bud left to develop

Right: Strong side shoots are produced as the result of early pinching out

The final objective: a plant which is short-jointed and produces side growth as near to soil level as possible

Suitable varieties for bedding. We have learnt from long experience that certain varieties are more tolerant than others of these conditions. The most famous bedding geranium is Paul Crampel, the original 'scarlet geranium'. This was introduced by Lemoine, in 1893, and has retained the public's affection ever since.

The colour, which is Dutch Vermilion, is rather strident, but Paul Crampel is extremely tough, and it will put up with the most adverse conditions to be found in industrial towns. Great care should be taken to get a true stock of this plant, as every inferior red single geranium is sold under its name. Fifty years ago it was to be seen everywhere with its traditional border of alternate white alyssum and blue lobelia, a truly patriotic gesture.

Just as Paul Crampel superseded Henry Jacoby, so has Paul Crampel been eclipsed in municipal favour by Gustav Emich. This old greenhouse variety is a softer colour than Paul Crampel and, being semi-double, it lasts longer. The plant, however, is rather large for bedding, and in a very wet season the flower heads tend to rot on the plant.

The double white variety Hermine is still grown widely, but if you must have a white geranium out of doors, the single Queen of the Whites is preferable. The salmon-pink King of Denmark is a semi-double, which is popular but more suitable for the greenhouse. The single cherry-red Doris Moore behaves well out of doors.

The ideal bedding geranium is a short-jointed, floriferous plant with flowers that do not shatter easily, and of a colour that is weatherproof. The orange variety Maxim Kovalevski does not really conform to these requirements, but its colour is so brilliant and unfailing that it is worth growing. The beautiful orange variety with a white eye, called Willingdon Gem in this country and Nouvelle Aurore in France, does not behave well out of doors in England, although it is used with great effect farther south in Europe.

The use of standard geraniums is a common practice in public parks, and it is possible to vary the colour effect with them. Gustav Emich is a very suitable variety for this purpose. A bed of the double geranium Royal Purple offers an unusual bedding display.

Certain types are suitable for edging purposes, the dwarf, variegated Madame Salleron, which never grows more than 6 in. high and does not flower, makes a distinctive border. The red- or pink-flowered Golden Harry Hieover is also dwarf and suitable for this purpose.

Many brilliant bedding effects can be obtained with the fancy-leaved section, where there are endless permutations of leaf colour and designs. The bronze and gold-leaved ones make a brave show. Caroline Schmidt and Mrs Parker give attractive silver foliage effects, and have pink and scarlet flowers.

The ivy-leaved pelargoniums are becoming fashionable as bedding plants. They are far less formal than zonals, and tend to cover more ground. One of the best varieties for this use is La France, with large lavender flowers.

Window-boxes. Geraniums are *par excellence* the plants for window-boxes, and provided they are kept adequately watered, they make a brave show. Very many are used for this purpose each year on shops, offices, and public buildings, to provide a welcome blaze of colour in the city streets.

Ivy-leaved pelargoniums can be made to trail over the edge of the window-box; an excellent variety for this purpose is the variegated L'Elégante. In Austria and Switzerland, every house seems to have window-boxes filled with colourful geraniums, and from the traditional Moorish balconies in Spain cascades of scarlet zonals and purple regals light up the narrow streets.

Urns and vases. Decorative urns and vases can be planted with trailing ivy-leaved varieties and in modern New Town centres austere concrete receptacles are massed with geraniums. The traditional Spanish garden consists of a paved courtyard, with large urns and jars which can be moved around. In Spain geraniums are used exclusively for this type of planting. This pattern of gardening is ideal for the town house, and geraniums are indispensable in this context.

Hanging baskets. Another way in which geraniums can be used decoratively is in hanging baskets. These are used where space is limited, or where the focus of colour is required at a higher point. Hanging baskets are often used in street decoration.

Soil and fertilisers. There is an old tradition that is hard to break, which implies that geraniums prefer a poor soil. It is true that, in the wild, they grow in near-desert conditions, but the modern cultivars prefer a fairly rich soil.

When a flower bed or window-box is being prepared for geraniums the soil should be well balanced, and with not too much nitrogenous material. For window-boxes, the John Innes Compost No. 2 is ideal. If the soil in the beds is clayey, coarse sharp sand and fibrous peat should be added to give a good soil structure. One of the proprietary fertilisers which are specially made for flowers may be added to the soil according to the manufacturer's directions.

If there is too much nitrogen in the soil, the plants will carry too much leaf, and the growth will be lush and sappy. Geraniums are extremely tolerant of most soils, and are not fussy about *p*H ratios, although a balance between *p*H 6 to 7 should be aimed at.

Time to plant. Geraniums for bedding are usually supplied in 3-inch pots, and the plant may very well be in flower at the time. The best period to plant out for either bedding or window-boxes is in late May, when in normal season there is no longer any danger of a frost. Many street traders, and some nursery shops, offer these plants in pots many weeks before the end of May. If they are put out in the open air, and there is a late frost, they will either be killed or severely damaged.

It is a good idea to harden off plants that have been received from a nurseryman in a cold frame. If these facilities are not available, they can stand out of doors in a sheltered position. The pots under these conditions should be well watered.

Planting. When the plants are ready for planting, they should be knocked out of their pots with the minimum of root disturbance. Allow plenty of space between the plants; 12 in. apart is by no means too much for a normal growing variety. Dwarf and slow-growing varieties can be set out in closer proximity. In fact, the excessively slow growing Mr Cox is often used with three plants set together. If there is no chance of immediate rain the newly planted geraniums should be well watered in.

It is important that the plants be firmed in very thoroughly, and short stakes may be necessary to support tender growth from the wind, and from the attentions of pets. This is particularly important where ivy-leaved varieties are being planted out.

After-care and maintenance. For the first few days the geranium will inevitably resent the process of replanting. This takes the form

27

of the yellowing of the lower leaves, and these should be removed at once. It is a good idea to remove also any large over-blown flower heads. Very soon, however, they will adjust themselves to their new conditions. It is essential that they do not lack water during this period and spraying the leaves in the evening during a dry period will also be beneficial.

The maintenance of geraniums thereafter consists in removing at weekly intervals all dead flower heads and yellowing leaves. It is very important to keep the plants shapely by pinching out any unwanted growths.

The surface soil should be well hoed, and weeds must be kept down. The only pest problems are the caterpillars of some tortrix moths, which eat the foliage. These are dealt with in Chapter 9.

Lifting. Once a stock of geraniums has been acquired, and provided over-wintering facilities are available, they will last for many years. The plants must be lifted before the first frosts of autumn. All long and straggling growth should be cut back to within 4 in. of soil level. Any long roots should be pruned off and the plants potted firmly in pots of the smallest size practicable. With proper care during the winter months, these plants may be used for bedding out the following season. I have used such plants for as long as eight consecutive years. The material which has been cut off may, of course, be used for taking cuttings.

To sum up, the success of the geranium in an outdoor bed depends largely on two factors: the variety used, and the weather conditions experienced during the growing season. The ideal bedding geranium is a short-jointed single or semi-double variety with the flowers— which should be weatherproof—held well above the foliage. Apart from ensuring that the geranium bed is in a position where it gets the maximum amount of sunlight, in this country we can do very little about the weather. An excessively wet season will produce rank growth, faded colours and mildewed flower heads. On the rare occasions when we have a hot, dry summer, the plants give of their best. Until one has seen the wealth of flower, and the intensity of colour of these plants growing in the Mediterranean littoral, one can have no idea of their decorative possibilities. However, we have adopted this African plant to our sunless climate, and it does its best for us.

28

CHAPTER FOUR

Greenhouse Cultivation

Sooner or later, the geranium enthusiast will find that he must have a heated greenhouse if he is to pursue his hobby satisfactorily and economically.

If cost is no object and geraniums are only to be used for bedding or window-box decoration plants may be bought in the spring and discarded in the autumn.

However, a great deal of the enjoyment in growing these plants is to be found in raising cuttings, and the building up of stocks of new or rare varieties. For this, the greenhouse is an indispensable aid. The type of greenhouse may be left to the discretion of the grower, but all the popular types in wood or metal are suitable for the cultivation of geraniums.

Heating of greenhouse. The heating of the greenhouse is important, as all frost must be excluded. On the other hand, geraniums do not require a temperature higher than 10°C. (50°F.). They will withstand greenhouse temperatures of over 38°C. (100°F.), but the object during the winter months is to maintain growth with the lowest possible expenditure on fuel.

The type of heating may be solid fuel, oil or electricity. For the amateur there is no doubt that electricity offers many advantages. Thermostats ensure than an even temperature is maintained, and the actual heating is most economically achieved by a combination of soil-heating and air-heating wires. Another modern method is the use of fan heaters, blowing warm air in the required direction. It is important to ask the advice of your local Electricity Board on these matters, for they will recommend the most suitable installation for your greenhouse.

Greenhouses heated by coke boilers are still largely used by commercial growers. They are economical but require attention during the night, and it is difficult to maintain a constant temperature with this type. Small oil-fired boilers are also available and are, of course, very labour-saving.

For a small greenhouse or lean-to, paraffin heaters may be used. Great care should be taken to avoid fumes, for some of these heaters pollute the atmosphere. Always use a paraffin heater which has been designed for the purpose.

Ventilation. It has been said that the secret of successful greenhouse management is not so much temperature control as atmosphere control. The great difficulty with all methods of heating is condensation. There is always water present in the soil in pots or in bench trays, and this evaporates into the warm air which rises until it meets the cold glass of the greenhouse where it condenses. It is important to have suitable ventilation so that this moist air may escape without undue loss of heat. A greenhouse, of course, is not the ideal type of construction for any type of heating. The large areas of glass offer many opportunities for loss of heat. Many gardeners overcome this problem by fitting an inner skin of polythene to their greenhouses.

Plants do not like unnatural draughts, but they do at the same time need a fairly constant circulation of air in order to thrive. Geraniums do not appreciate a stagnant, humid atmosphere. The electrical blower heaters have gone a long way towards solving this problem without an extravagant loss of heat.

Shading. There is no doubt that all types of geraniums are seen at their best under glass. Yet there is a limit to the amount of concentrated sunlight which they can take in a greenhouse. Although blinds are not necessary, a light application of a shading compound should be applied to the glass by the end of April. In a particularly sunny season, this may have to be renewed before the end of the season.

Cleanliness. During the winter months, the glass should be kept as clear as possible, in order to obtain the maximum sunlight. Condensation, of course, obscures the light and encourages the formation of algae on the glass.

One of the cardinal principles of greenhouse management is cleanliness. The sheltered atmosphere provides a perfect breeding ground for all types of pests and diseases. Once a year, at least, the greenhouse should be emptied of plants, scrubbed out with a solution of a disinfectant, such as formaldehyde, and repainted if necessary. The wood must be examined for rotting, and all the crannies and crevices must be thoroughly cleaned out. If gravel or sand is used on the staging, this must be washed and sterilised.

The leaves of plants must be kept free of dirt and deposits by spraying them frequently, and the surface soil in the pots should be regularly broken up, to prevent it becoming sour and moss growing on it.

Pots. Many types of receptacle have been tried for geraniums, and there is no doubt that the clay pot is the cheapest and the most successful. Plastic containers are much lighter and retain moisture for longer periods, but good clay pots which are scrupulously clean, both inside and out, allow the roots to breathe. New earthenware pots, when first received from the shops, should be thoroughly soaked in water before being used.

Size of pots. One of the commonest mistakes made by the amateur is to over-pot. Cuttings should be started in a 2-inch pot, and then transferred to a 3-inch pot when they have filled the smaller pot with roots.

For greenhouse work, and taking the average type of young zonal or regal pelargonium, a 4½-inch pot is adequate for flowering purposes. Naturally a miniature will be happy permanently in a 3-inch pot, whereas a very strongly growing double will require a 6-inch pot, or even larger, to give of its best.

Composts. When greenhouse varieties arrive from the nurseryman, they are usually packed in paper or whalehide containers, and should be transferred as soon as possible to clay pots. The most suitable compost is John Innes No. 1 potting compost. Many inferior and inaccurate mixtures are offered by dealers as the genuine John Innes compost, and care should be taken to purchase your potting medium from a reputable nurseryman.

A new type of loamless potting compost is now available. This consists of finely granulated peat and sand, with no other ingredient apart from a base fertiliser. Geraniums will grow in this mixture, but I do not think it has any advantages over the more conventional composts. In addition there is the fact that if it is allowed to dry out the powdery black peat tends to be watered out of the pots.

After-care. When the pots have been crocked and a little compost placed on top, the plants should be firmed in thoroughly with the fingers and the soil levelled off to within one inch of the top of the pot. The plant should then be well watered. Some yellowing of the lower leaves will inevitably take place, and they should be removed. It is advisable to place the newly potted plants in a shaded position for a few days, until the plants have had a chance to establish themselves.

If the leaves continue to turn yellow after two weeks, it is obvious that the plant is unhappy in its present environment. The most common cause of failure in this instance is over-watering. Very often an amateur gardener will stand his pots in saucers or receptacles full of water and the roots are literally drowned for lack of air.

Geraniums will do very well if the pots are stood on open slatted staging, although some people prefer to plunge the pots in sand, gravel or peat, up to half their height.

Feeding. Plants in pots require feeding if they are to give good results. And although the John Innes composts contain a base fertiliser, this is soon exhausted by the plant. Briefly, the plants need phosphates for root growth, nitrates for the production of leaves, and potash for flowers and fruit. A balance of these three elements is conveniently supplied in proprietary mixtures, of which there are many suitable for flowering plants.

The fertiliser should be applied at the rates and time intervals recommended by the manufacturers. If the plant is making rapid growth, or is transferred to a larger pot, the feed can be increased slightly, but the application of excessive amounts of chemical fertilisers can damage the roots of the plants and is, of course, wasteful. Never attempt to top-feed a dry plant; it should always be well watered first.

If the fancy-leaved geraniums are being grown in the greenhouse, it is advisable to give them less water, and feeding must be withheld, or confined to mixtures without nitrogen. This will give a much greater intensity of colour to the leaves. Over-feeding of these varieties makes the leaves grow out of their brighter colours.

LEAF-AXIL CUTTINGS

A suitable shoot
with bud and leaf

A cut is made
$\frac{1}{4}$ in. below the
joint

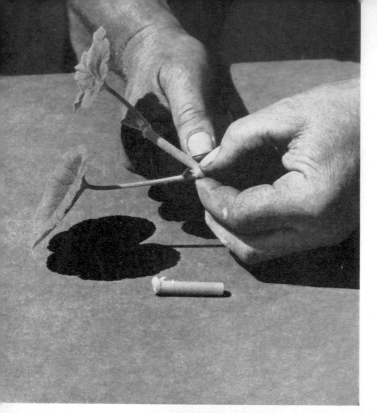

Another cut $\frac{1}{4}$ in. above the bud

A section of stem with one bud and one leaf

A vertical cut is
made through the
stem . . .

. . . making sure
the bud and leaf
are intact

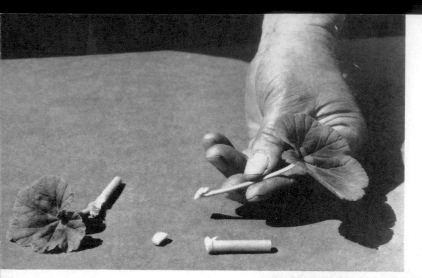

The finished cutting

Inserting the cutting gently

Firming in so that the bud is just covered

Spacing. The arrangement of the pots in the greenhouse is important, and overcrowding must be avoided. It must be remembered that a small zonal or regal will grow into a tall, straggling plant in one season, and it is essential to give the plants room to expand. Adequate light and space are essential during the growing season, although during the winter resting plants may be packed together more closely.

Standards. The production of standard geraniums can be carried out in the greenhouse. The more vigorous zonals are usually preferred for this work. A leading growth is selected and all other growing points are removed. The stem can be kept straight by binding it at intervals to a cane. The aim is to secure a sturdy 3-foot stem. When the required height has been reached, this single growing tip is pinched out, to encourage side shoots at the top of the stem. This normally takes two growing seasons. A stake is essential at all times. The plants usually selected for this purpose are Gustav Emich, Decorator, and Hermine.

The possibilities of grafting a less vigorous variety are dealt with in Chapter 5. One or two standards in the greenhouse will add variety to the layout. The scented-leaved red variety Crispum Varigatum can be trained into a cypress-shaped bush.

One such specimen was exhibited at the Geranium Society's competition in 1957 by Mr Parrett. It was 3 feet high and perfectly symmetrical. It was awarded a cup by the Geranium Society (now the British Pelargonium and Geranium Society) and the Royal Horticultural Society awarded it a Certificate of Cultural Commendation. In describing how this magnificent specimen geranium was grown, Mr Parrett stated that he took a cutting in July, 1955. By November his cutting had been potted on into a 5-inch pot. It was stood on a pedestal, and turned every day. By February, the plant was big enough for a 7-inch pot. It was fed with well-rotted pig manure. By August, 1956, it was 30 inches high. It was fed with nitrate of potash and coaxed with the fingers into producing one growing tip. By November, 1956, it had been hard pruned at the sides and repotted into a 10-inch pot. It grew on well until April, 1957, when it was shaped by hand, and ready for showing.

Continual flowering. One of the great advantages of a greenhouse is that it is possible to have geraniums in flower during twelve months of the year. This is particularly the case with certain zonal varieties. Regals have a flowering period from April onwards until the middle of September, but, in the main, zonals do not appear to have any set dormant period.

Winter flowering. It is worth while growing plants specially for winter display. Cuttings are taken in the spring, and are grown on vigorously during the summer. All the flower buds must be removed until the end of September. The plants will then go ahead and produce flowers for at least four months. Unless temperatures of up to 16°C. (60°F.) can be maintained, and there is plenty of light, the development of the flower heads will be much slower.

Some pink varieties such as King of Denmark have certain colour changes when they flower in the winter. The reddish colour tends to move towards the centre, leaving a white edge to the petals. As a general rule, singles and semi-doubles do better than the fully-double varieties, and particularly the rose-bud kinds.

Among the more reliable sorts for this work are the following: Maxime Kovalevski, Dryden, Lady Warwick, E. Hockey, Willingdon Beauty, Caledonia, and Countess of Jersey. The question of improving the flowering of these zonals with the help of artificial light has never been fully explored, but future research will undoubtedly show results. It may well be that regals, which produce flowers during the longest days of the year, can be influenced to flower during the winter.

The geranium can be rapidly propagated in a greenhouse for summer bedding. Cuttings taken in the autumn can be overwintered, and grown for outside planting. The methods of propagation are dealt with in Chapter 6.

Regals for summer flowering. It is, of course, with regals that the summer greenhouse display can make its most extravagant show. Regals are rarely used out of doors in this country. If you have the space, regal pelargoniums can be grown in pots into plants up to 5 feet in diameter, and bearing up to one hundred and fifty trusses of magnificent flowers. From cuttings taken in mid-July, the centre of the plant must be kept continually pinched out, as most regals tend to run up into a long, straggling plant. The aim is to secure a short, stocky plant, with as many branches coming from as near the base as possible. Regals will not tolerate damp, hot conditions, and they must be grown hard.

Some of the new American regals have a much dwarfer growth, but some of the large specimen plants which are shown at the exhibitions of the Royal Horticultural Society are magnificent. Cultivars such as Carisbrooke, Caprice, Lord Bute and Carnival are outstanding.

It is important to ripen the wood, if one is to have a good flush of flowers; and in addition to taking cuttings from stock plants grown in the open garden, during the winter and early spring the pots should be placed as near to the glass as possible.

CHAPTER FIVE

Geraniums as House Plants

The possibilities of using geraniums in living rooms have never been thoroughly explored. These plants were the favourites for the parlour windows of old country cottages, where they may still be seen crowding the window panes with leaf and colour. Many of our lost or long-forgotten varieties have been discovered by enthusiasts in this way.

In Scandinavia, geraniums are used among all the exotic range of house plants that are grown in those countries, to give colour in the winter months. In Germany, regal pelargoniums are sold in the spring as commonly as Indian azaleas.

Conditions for growing indoors. As anyone who has successfully grown a collection of plants in a living room knows, there are certain essential requirements. Apart from the long-suffering aspidistra, the rubber plant (*Ficus elastica decora*) and *Cissus antarctica*, room plants require a moist growing atmosphere, plenty of light, and the minimum extremes of temperature.

Central heating solves the latter problem, but it does make the atmosphere too dry for plant growth. This is normally overcome by setting the pots in trays of pebbles or gravel, which are kept moist. It is not enough for the plants to be well watered, the atmosphere immediately surrounding them must also be moist.

The only part of most living rooms which is light enough to grow geraniums successfully is the window-sill, and in many houses this is the draughtiest and coldest part of the room.

We know that geraniums are the most versatile and good-tempered of plants. Provided they are not frost-bitten, they will survive a multitude of indignities. To get the best from them, and to secure with some zonal pelargoniums an almost continuous succession of bloom, they must have good treatment.

Care of geraniums indoors. Give them the sunniest position, and keep the centre of the plant well pinched out. Remove all dead and fading flower heads and syringe the leaves frequently with clean water. Dust is always settling inside houses, and this clogs the pores of the leaves. Do not stand the pots in saucers of stagnant water, as the soil in the pots will go sour and the leaves on the plant turn yellow. This is the commonest cause of failure.

Suitable types. Ivy-leaved geraniums are often used in America for training around the window frame, but it must be remembered that ivy-leaved varieties do not normally flower in the winter months. Regal pelargoniums may be used for house decoration, but it is better to bring them in from the greenhouse when they are in bud, and to rest the plants out of doors when the flowering season is over.

Fancy-leaved and scented-leaved geraniums offer endless decorative possibilities. It should be remembered that the varieties with more brightly coloured leaves need rather drier conditions than other zonals, if they are to give of their best in regard to colour.

Cut flowers. Another way in which these plants may be used indoors is as cut flowers. Apart from certain single-flowered types, semi-double and double flowers will last in water for many weeks and can provide a touch of brilliant colour during the winter months. The foliage of so widely varying a family offers endless variations for floral decorations, for the dining room or other parts of the house. In a small greenhouse, it is possible to provide enough flowers and foliage to have a floral decoration in the home every month of the year.

Queen Victoria used geraniums and maidenhair ferns as a table decoration, and there is no doubt that this charming addition to a well-loaded table would appeal to modern hostesses. The colours of many zonal and regal flowers are particularly attractive under artificial light, and have a luminous quality which is not detected in daylight.

CHAPTER SIX

Propagation from Cuttings

The principal method of propagation is by cuttings. The geranium is a most accommodating plant in this respect. *Pelargonium tetragonum* is an interesting example of this method of increase in the wild, where small branches fall to the ground and take root. The grower who wishes to increase his stock of a particular plant can take a stem cutting and root it.

Ideal cutting. Cutting may be taken at any time of the year, but spring and autumn would appear to be the most suitable times. The ideal cutting should have three joints, and it is better to have a short-jointed piece than a long one. When looking for suitable shoots from which to make cuttings, it must be remembered that we are also pruning the plant. The actual point at which the roots will grow is the joint or node, so that the cutting should be trimmed with a very sharp knife just below the node. The stipules should be carefully removed, and all leaves except two or three at the top of the cutting should be removed. If too many leaves are left, the cutting will soon droop and die.

Inserting cuttings. If you are using the right sort of compost, it will not be necessary to use a dibber, and the procedure is to push the end of the cutting down into the soil. There is no need to use hormone rooting preparations, as cuttings from most types of geraniums will begin rooting almost at once.

Six cuttings may be placed around the edge of a 5-inch pot, or firmed into boxes. One of the main causes of failure with geranium cuttings is black-leg, a fungus disease which may be encouraged by over-watering of the cuttings, or the infection being carried from one plant to another by the knife. It is most important to ensure that the knife-blade is disinfected after each cut.

Time taken to root. The time taken for a geranium cutting to root depends upon the time of year and the variety which is being propagated. Under favourable conditions, the roots may be growing strongly in two weeks, and the pots may be full of roots in six weeks. The trouble is that some miniature and short-jointed plants produce very little material for propagation, and the cuttings themselves take much longer to root.

Thin-stemmed varieties. Ivy-leaved varieties with their thinner stems tend to snap off at the joints. Cuttings, however, should be taken a little below the joint, and they appear to take root more readily in September than at any other time. The procedure with scented-leaved varieties is similar. In the rare cases where the plant produces underground tubers, they may be easily separated and replanted. Other sorts which are virtually stemless are propagated by root cuttings.

Stock plants. The normal life of a geranium plant is about six years, and if it has been regularly pruned back it will have produced dozens of new plants from cuttings. All these plants which have been propagated vegetatively are, of course, identical to the parent and are, in effect, part of the mother plant. It is important therefore to buy plants, in the first instance, from a specialist grower who makes sure that his stock plants are true to name. This is particularly true in the case of the zonal pelargonium Paul Crampel, when almost any single red geranium, many of them stray seedlings, is wrongly sold under this name.

Mist propagation. Geraniums have been found to respond well to increase by mist propagation. Briefly, with this method of propagation the cuttings are placed in trays of sand, provided with bottom-heat by means of soil-heating cables. Spray nozzles are inserted in the sand, about 18 inches above the plant. As soon as the atmosphere over the plants becomes dry, a valve is opened on each nozzle and a fine mist is produced for a few seconds. The sprays are then automatically cut off until the atmosphere becomes dry again.

This controlled environment of bottom-heat and fine spray induces the most difficult plants to root easily. With geraniums it greatly speeds up propagation and this method is now used by many commercial growers who can produce saleable plants rapidly, as the orders come in.

It is very successful with regals, where the cuttings are often woody. Small installations are now available for the amateur through the horticultural trade.

Cullus formation. Some growers have found that cuttings which have been left on the bench do not die off, and tend to form a protective skin over the cut end; they recommend that all cuttings should be treated in this way. There is no evidence to support the theory that cuttings so dried off will produce better plants more quickly, but it says a very great deal for the tenacity of life of the plant that will tolerate these conditions.

Some gardeners still persist in digging up their geraniums in the autumn and hanging them up by the roots in a frost-proof shed or cellar. In the past when this practice was carried out these straggly, leafless plants—or at any rate those which had escaped frost and mildew—were then set out in the garden early in the year. Many of them did survive, and may do so today, but it is not a method to be recommended. The plants take a very long time to recover, and they will never make shapely plants.

Leaf-axil cuttings. In recent years, a new system of propagation has been developed by Mr L. A. Foote, called 'leaf-bud cuttings', or more correctly 'leaf-axil cuttings'. His method is to take sections one-quarter-of-an-inch above and below a node, and then cut each nodal section vertically between the buds. Thus, the cutting consists of about three-quarters-of-an-inch of stem split through the middle, with each section containing a bud and leaf.

These small cuttings are then inserted upright in a box of compost. Forty-eight cuttings can be contained in one seed tray. The appearance of the tray is of a collection of geranium leaves facing in one direction, and inclined at an angle. It is important to ensure that each axil contains a bud.

Actual rooting is slower with this method, but it enables the grower to take many more cuttings, and to produce plants which are short-jointed from the start. Mr Foote has used this method at the Beckenham Parks Department for some time, with great success. A combination of leaf axil cuttings and mist propagation might very well be tried.

Zonal pelargonium: Harlow Pearl, white with a very slight tinge of magenta

Zonal pelargonium: Dolly Varden, a silver tricolor

Zonal pelargonium:
Masterpiece, a bronze and
gold-leaved variety

Zonal pelargonium:
Mrs Quilter, also a
bronze and gold-leaved
variety

Zonal pelargonium: Distinction, a black-leaved variety with cherry-coloured flowers

Zonal pelargonium:
Mr Henry Cox, a popular
golden tricolor

Zonal pelargonium:
Jenifer, a miniature
variety

Grafting. This is another method of increasing a choice but weak variety, using a more vigorous stock. The methods employed are similar to those used for tree grafting, and some of the most successful results have been obtained by grafting a slow-growing, fancy-leaved variety on to a more vigorous stem. There is no evidence that this method could be carried out on a commercial scale.

Root cuttings. It has been discovered that root cuttings are more successful with regals than with geraniums belonging to other sections. Root cuttings do not necessarily come true to parent, and it has been said that many fancy-leaved geraniums produce yellow-leaved plants from root cuttings.

The method is to remove the soil from the roots of a mature plant, and cut the roots in lengths of one inch, or a little longer. These are buried in compost in a seed tray to a depth of one-quarter-of-an-inch. The box should then be placed in a propagating frame. Shoots appear in two months, and should be thinned out to one shoot per cutting.

CHAPTER SEVEN

Propagation from Seed

One of the more adventurous ways of growing geraniums is to propagate them from seed. As the geranium is a much hybridised plant, it follows that unless the seed comes from true species it will not reproduce the same plant as the parents. Geraniums do not produce an enormous amount of seed, but each single seed is extremely well equipped for survival. In fact, each flower produces only five seeds, packed in the long, pointed 'storksbill' container. When the seed is ripe, the carpels split off. The carpel itself, which remains attached to the seed, is twisted like a spring and acts in two ways. Firstly, it acts as a parachute, and secondly, when the seed has been blown by the wind, the spiral tail alternately twists and straightens with changes in atmosphere. The seed is thereby screwed into the ground by the action of this highly modified carpel.

Natural pollination. Although only one or two seeds in each beak are fertile, nature ensures a high rate of germination in a dry and rocky terrain. In addition, the geranium has a natural protection against self-pollination, for the pollen in one flower is ripe before the stigma in that flower is ready to use it. In the wild, geraniums are pollinated by lepidoptera and other insects, and this process is assisted by the colour of the flowers themselves, and the markings of the petals. In some cases the flowers are heavily scented in the evening to attract the moths.

Unknown seedlings. A good deal of geranium or pelargonium seed is offered by various dealers. This is often collected from plants growing in the Mediterranean area, in a semi-wild state. It is never likely to produce plants of any quality. Geranium seedlings are often sold in the spring, but unless the parentage is known, the plants will usually be worthless. Many of them will never flower at all, and others, after a long period of growth, will only produce insignificant

42

flower-heads. After a lapse of many years, fine quality, hand-pollinated seed is now being offered for sale, but it is, of course, expensive.

Selecting parents. The procedure for pollination is governed by the choice of plant, and the grower must have a clear idea in his mind of the sort of new break at which he is aiming. It is as well to remember that with the exception of the true species, most of the plants available for breeding purposes are of extremely mixed and complicated ancestry. It is rare for us to be able to forecast the results of cross-pollination. In the case of the variety Harlow Pearl, the pale mauve single variety Caledonia was crossed with the single Queen of the Whites, to produce a cultivar with the best qualities of both parents. In the bud, Harlow Pearl is flushed with pink, but the perfectly formed open flower is a silvery, pearly grey. It has the distinctive orange stamens of Queen of the Whites.

When the plants have been chosen, it is important that the flowers of the plant to bear the seed should be older than those of the plant selected for its pollen. The female flower head should be reduced to a few florets and then covered with a polythene or muslin bag, to prevent the intrusion of unwanted insects. When dry pollen can be seen on the male plant, a very small sterile camel-hair brush should be applied to the ends of the stamens. Removing the bag from the female plant, this pollen is then applied to the stigma of each floret and the protective cover replaced. Only long experience can determine when both plants are at the stage for this procedure.

Seed formation and sowing. As soon as the seed vessels are seen to be forming, the bag should be removed, so that the seed can ripen. A careful watch must be kept on the seed-pods, otherwise the seeds will be projected all over the greenhouse.

The seed is said to be viable for several years, but the best results are obtained if it is sown as soon as possible. The feathery tails should be removed and the seeds should be individually placed in pans. Germination normally takes place within fourteen days, and occurs most favourably between 10 and 13°C. (50 and 55°F.).

Registration of new plants. The seedlings should have their central stems pinched out, and it may be many months before the

43

flowers appear. All worthless or duplicate kinds should be discarded as soon as they flower. Many so-called new named varieties are produced from seed every year by amateurs and nurserymen. They make no effort to ascertain whether their prized new seedlings already exist under old-established names. It is strongly recommended that all new seedlings should be submitted to the council of The British Pelargonium and Geranium Society for registration. The council will tell the grower if the variety is worth propagating, and, of course, will ensure the best financial return for any outstanding new breaks.

Blue pelargoniums. There are many people in this country, as well as in America and Australia, searching for new varieties of merit. A hundred years ago, the search was for a truly blue geranium. There are, of course, many varieties of hardy blue geraniums to be found in the rock garden or herbaceous border, and there have been advertisements offering for sale hardy blue geraniums which can be left out all the year. Gardeners who expect to receive a new type of zonal pelargonium which is not only hardy but also possesses blue flowers will be sadly disappointed. This is looking a long way into the future.

Sporting. Many new varieties are not the result of cross-pollination at all but arise from 'sporting'. This occurs when a cultivar produces a branch which is unlike the rest of the plant. It is well known that many of the choicest new zonals were discovered in this way. Occasionally, a zonal plant will produce a pure white shoot, which is devoid of chlorophyll. This shoot will continue to flourish as long as it is attached to the parent plant, but as soon as it is removed it will die. Certain silver-leaved varieties produce sports which are reversions to plain green-leaved ancestors. Sometimes the sport has flowers of a different colour or form, and it is likely that the semi-doubles and cactus varieties arose in this way.

When large numbers of geraniums are grown commercially, or in parks, the opportunities for finding sports are frequent. We can do nothing with our present knowledge to induce a geranium to sport, when it has no inclination to do so. This is the luck of the draw, and the man with a few common varieties in his modest lean-to is just as likely to discover a valuable sport as the expert who is searching for them among thousands of show plants.

Provided the sporting branch is considered worth propagating for leaf colour or flower colour, it may be detached and grown on as a cutting.

One of the common sorts which tends to sport is Madame Salleron, which is a flowerless silver-leaved miniature; this often throws a taller form with an entirely different leaf-form, and carrying small pink flowers. This sport has been fixed and is known as Little Trot or Mrs Newton. The variegated ivy-leaved L'Élégante often sports a wholly green-leaved variety.

The old variety Vesuvius has produced many widely varying sports, and more recently the orange single Maxim Kovalevski produced a sport called Salmon Kovalevski.

CHAPTER EIGHT

The Search for New Varieties

The ancestry of many new geraniums is obscure, but in the July, 1952, bulletin of the Geranium Society (the present British Pelargonium and Geranium Society) Mr E. Humphris has tried to clarify the parentage of the zonal pelargonium Elizabeth Cartwright. He states that the first parents were Paul Crampel and Henry Jacoby. He thinks that it also has Banbury Cross among its parents. The new variety was given an Award of Merit in 1950 by the Royal Horticultural Society and was later awarded the Sander Medal as the best new greenhouse plant of the year.

Elizabeth Cartwright consists of a fusion of two red tones, Cherry Red and Dutch Vermilion, with a small white eye, but as Derek Clifford points out, it is not very different from a variety called Aldenham, which was certainly in cultivation by 1900, or the famous Mrs Eddowes, which is even older. In any case all three varieties are difficult growers and prone to disease and distortion.

It is unfortunate that many of the rarest and most unusual geraniums are the most temperamental to grow. The beautiful Trésor is a case in point. One is always searching for a fresh stock of this elegant and desirable flower. It is double, of pale pinkish-orange colouring, flaked with creamy white, and is one of the rarest colour forms. But it is a cripple, and as soon as it is growing away vigorously, it produces monstrous fasciated growths. The leaves and stem are subject to corky excrescences.

Of new miniature varieties with coloured leaves and large double flowers, outstanding are Carolyn, with small dark leaves and very large pink flowers, and White Gem, the first white miniature. In regals the field is wide and the possibilities of new colour breaks are very encouraging.

An outstanding introduction in 1956 was Silver Kewense, which arose as a sport from *P. kewense*. A slight edging of white appeared on one leaf. This was then grown on and propagated for three years, when it was launched on the market. Although it has similar flowers to its parent, it is much smaller in growth. From the same source, a well-known geranium nursery, came four miniature black-leaved varieties—Tiberius, Claudius, Nero and one with double pink flowers, Timothy Clifford. This nursery was also responsible for the reintroduction and renaming of many lost varieties. This is particularly the case with the species which require expert knowledge and research before they can be named. Another specialist geranium nursery makes valuable contributions by its own new varieties, and by their introductions from Switzerland and Czechoslovakia. These include Orangesonne, from Switzerland, which has turned out to be the best double orange bedder plant. Whereas the colours of these new mid-European varieties are not so very different, they have a more compact form than existing varieties.

Another outstanding introduction was the famous Willingdon Gem, a large single orange zonal, with a fine white eye. Mr W. A. R. Clifton's crimson bedding variety Doris Moore appeared as a sport from Charles Blair. Yet another superb Clifton variety is Victorious, a kind of super Paul Crampel. Unfortunately this variety has a tendency to revert to a smaller flower.

On the whole, the ivy-leaved section and the fancy-leaved group have been the most neglected, although a Californian grower has been prominent with new ivy-leaved pelargoniums. Among these are Butterflies, with large, single, purple flowers; The Duchess, with white, double flowers, striped and blotched with purple; Jester, another double, pale purple; and El Gaucho, another double purple.

Some fancy-leaved varieties have been introduced from America, including Lady Luck, a new butterfly-leaved kind, and S. A. Nutt, a silver-leaved variety. Jane Maxwell is a golden tricolor. The enormous duplication of names still requires a great deal of sorting out.

Peter Grieve spent over fifteen years from 1854 onwards working on these plants, and raised dozens of decorative-foliaged pelargoniums. Unfortunately, there are in existence few accurate colour illustrations, and we can only guess at the colours and markings of the original plants. From 1860 onwards hundreds of bronze-zoned were listed, but only a doubtful dozen can be traced today. A list such as the *Cannell Floral Guide* for 1910 describes ten varieties with double flowers, of which only three appear to be in cultivation at the present time. Sometimes details are given, but such descriptions as 'well known', 'a gem' and 'grand variety' are no help at all.

Some of these varieties may still exist in old greenhouse collections, and every year some new claimant to a venerable name is submitted for inspection. The possibilities for the amateur are endless. Detective work when travelling abroad, or in this country, is fruitful. In the past most of the brilliant new varieties in this section were produced from seedlings, and there are many opportunities here for the amateur.

A pure yellow-leaved variety with clear rose-pink flowers called Golden Crest has been raised here, and an introduction from the United States called Medallion has a trifid leaf with a bronze mark in the centre, and pink flowers. Miss Mary Campbell has produced another golden-leaved variety with the advantage of soft pink and cream flowers.

One of the most striking new fancy-leaved geraniums is the dwarf silver-leaved Madame Butterfly. This outstanding introduction has double, dark red flowers, and the leaves have a dark green marking on a white base.

Zonal pelargonium:
Opal, a miniature variety

Zonal pelargonium:
Red Black Vesuvius, a
miniature with black leaves

Zonal pelargonium:
Madame Salleron, a silver-
leaved miniature which
does not flower

Zonal pelargonium:
Silver Kewense, also a silver-
leaved miniature

CHAPTER NINE

Pests and Diseases

On the whole the geranium family is not particularly subject to the attacks of insect pests. Different types of geranium may be attacked in individual ways. Zonal pelargoniums are, in the main, immune to the attacks of greenfly or aphids. Regal pelargoniums, on the other hand, are unfortunately plagued by whitefly.

With regard to greenhouse cultivation, it must be remembered that plants which are unhealthy are far more liable to infestation than strong-growing ones, and it is of the greatest importance to keep the greenhouse as clean as possible. All rubbish should be removed from the house at frequent intervals, as this is a breeding ground for many types of pests and disorders.

Aphids. These creatures live by sucking the sap from leaves and buds, causing the growth to become either stunted or distorted. In addition, aphids are often the carriers of virus infection from one plant to another. As I have said, they will leave zonal pelargoniums severely alone, especially if there are ivy-leaved, scented, or regal pelargoniums around. It must be remembered that they increase at a tremendous rate, and it is essential to deal with them as soon as they are found. They congregate on the underside of young, tender leaves and rapidly spread to all parts of the house.

Many types of proprietary preparations are on the market to control this pest, but since we are dealing with the greenhouse, which can be sealed, fumigation is by far the best method. The use of nicotine is a sure method of killing greenfly. Nicotine liquid concentrate may be poured into a metal saucer and heated by a spirit lamp. The vapour is given off and fills the house, penetrating into every crevice. As nicotine is an extremely dangerous poison, a safer way of using this valuable substance is to use fumigating shreds, which are sold by various makers. These shreds are lighted and give off smoke which is heavily impregnated with nicotine. It is very

D

important to keep well away from the greenhouse when it is full of poisonous fumes, and care should be taken when clearing the house to see that the fumes do not enter domestic quarters.

Certain smoke bombs containing DDT and BHC together may be used but so far nothing has proved as effective as nicotine. Many commercial growers use an Aerovap; this is an electrical apparatus which gives off small quantities of insecticide into the air continuously. It should be noted that DDT smokes on their own do not control aphids.

Malathion, applied as a spray or dust, will give an adequate control over aphids, and will also kill leaf miners, leaf-hoppers and thrips; it will also partly control whitefly and red spider.

A combination of lindane and DDT smokes are non-poisonous, and available to amateurs; they control aphids, caterpillars, capsids and woodlice, among other pests.

Whitefly. A whitefly infestation is very difficult to detect, but if the plants are brushed with the hand, and tiny white flying particles are seen fluttering around the plant, you will know that you have a visit from this unwelcome pest. Regal pelargoniums are particularly prone to attack by these creatures. DDT, applied as a smoke, is the most effective means of control, but malathion may also be used, as stated above, if other pests need to be controlled as well. This pest is one of the most difficult to eradicate as it breeds very rapidly. If you grow a large number of regals, it is important to keep a constant watch for whitefly. A bad attack results in the foliage becoming sticky and mottled. Fumigating at 14-day intervals is recommended if you have an attack in the greenhouse.

Red spider. The red spider is not a spider at all, but a mite, which is very difficult to see with the naked eye. Groups may be seen as reddish patches, usually on the underside of leaves. The symptoms are a drying up of the leaves of geraniums, particularly the ivy-leaved varieties. These pests multiply rapidly and are extremely difficult to eradicate.

Red spider mites thrive in a hot, dry atmosphere, and do not like a greenhouse where the air is kept humid. Commercial growers are more likely to be troubled by this pest than the amateur. A sure method of prevention is to keep the greenhouse cool and moist during the summer months, and to make sure that there is no litter on the floors, or in crevices where the mites can lurk.

The control of this pest has to ensure that both eggs and adult stages are killed. Azobenzene, which is non-poisonous, controls the egg stage but only a proportion of the adult stage, and professional growers use a smoke containing both azobenzene and parathion. Unfortunately parathion is poisonous and preparations containing it are not available to amateurs. For amateurs, azobenzene smoke is recommended for the control of red spider and two applications should be given with a ten-day interval.

The characteristic rusty patch which indicates the presence of red spider should not be confused with a corky excrescence, which is also liable to affect the undersides of the leaves of the ivy-leaved group as well as certain zonals. This blemish does not seem to be caused by a fungus or a parasitic creature, but appears to be a malformation of the cells.

Caterpillars. These pests are mainly the larvae of certain tortrix moths and not the larvae of butterflies as was suggested by one authority. Even the common Cabbage White can be encouraged to fly around your geraniums. They will certainly not lay their eggs on this plant. Caterpillars may be controlled by DDT smokes, or by one of the well-known sprays.

All butterflies, moths, bees, and flies should be excluded from the greenhouse if you are growing plants for seed. Bees are the worst offenders and industriously pollinate all the flowers in the greenhouse.

Virus. This disease is the one most dreaded by all pelargonium growers. Quite suddenly a perfectly healthy plant shows spotting on the leaf, and in later stages the leaves are swollen and distorted. It takes a very practised eye to detect virus in its early stages, and although in a commercial house full of one variety the infected plants will stand out, in a house of many different varieties the disorder goes unnoticed at first.

There is no cure, and as soon as this condition is detected the entire plant must be burnt. It is said that all geraniums have some form of virus, latent or otherwise, and it is true that some plants appear to grow out of it. The only precautions that one can take are to purchase plants from reputable growers, and to ensure the most hygienic conditions possible in the greenhouse. It is obvious that the disease can be spread by taking cuttings from diseased plants. Great care should be taken in any case to sterilise the instrument used for taking cuttings.

Botrytis. *Botrytis cinerea* or grey mould will often attack geraniums in damp, badly ventilated conditions. This disease will attack double varieties out of doors in a wet season. The months of October and November are the danger months in the greenhouse. The typical furry growth or mould spots appear on flowers or leaves.

There is no necessity to take special measures against this type of fungus except to maintain a correct greenhouse atmosphere, and to remove any affected parts of the plant. For heavy attacks a proprietary fungicide containing thiram may be used.

Black-leg. This disease, which is sometimes called black rot, or pelargonium stem rot, is probably caused by a species of *Fusarium*, although some authorities claim that it is a type of *Pythium*. Unfortunately, most growers of pelargoniums are likely to meet this trouble.

It generally appears soon after cuttings have been taken. The lower part of the stem, particularly at ground level, turns black. The infection spreads up the stem and soon kills it. It can also attack established plants. If the trouble is noticed in its early stages, it is possible to cut off the diseased portion, making sure that there are no signs of discoloration in the core of the stem. The cutting may then be replanted.

Although very little research has been carried out on pelargonium black leg, it seems certain that the infection is encouraged in two ways. One of the most important preventive measures is to make sure that the soil where the cuttings are growing is not too wet, and that the atmosphere is not too humid. Another source of infection is damage to the skin of the stem, and it is important that a clean cut is made, every time with a sharp, sterile knife. This trouble is most prevalent with soft, sappy cuttings.

A grower has recently experimented with smearing petroleum jelly on the ends of cuttings to avoid the disease. He claims a high percentage of success.

Leaf-spotting. Not all leaf discoloration is due to virus. Over-watering can produce this effect, and dead petals falling on the leaf give this effect. Sun-scorch can also produce a mottled effect, or it may be some mineral deficiency in the potting soil.

Reddening of the leaves is usually the result of a violent change of temperature. If plants have been bedded out before the cold nights are over, an intense reddening of the leaves will be seen. This will usually clear up under the right conditions.

Distortion. These malformations include a sudden thickening or even a 'twinning' of the main stem. Certain varieties are very prone to this, especially the rarer kinds. The flower-heads may be fasciated in this instance and should be removed.

Another malformation is an unnatural stunted growth of cells springing from the base of the plant. These blind vegetable excres-cences should be removed. It is possible to propagate perfectly healthy cuttings provided they are not taken from the affected part of the plant.

Another type of distortion is in the flower-head of the single varieties where further peduncles are produced, projecting flowers beyond the normal truss. These should be removed as soon as they appear, as they do not improve the form of the flower.

These distortions of cell growth must inevitably arise in a plant as in-bred and over-hybridised as the geranium. However they will only appear occasionally and do not cause a great deal of trouble.

CHAPTER TEN

Growing for Show

The geranium is an extremely easy and good-tempered plant to grow. It will not be a tragedy if the greenhouse is left unattended for a few days, as the plants can endure conditions of extreme heat and lack of water without suffering ill-effects. As we have seen, geraniums are among the easiest of all plants to propagate, and it is perhaps for these reasons that many are so badly grown.

It should be the aim of every grower to get the best out of his plants. Among such a wide field many thousands of sports are offered by nurserymen. It pays the enthusiast to specialise in one section.

Local horticultural societies usually have a class for pot plants, and it is in this section that geraniums are normally shown. The British Pelargonium and Geranium Society holds an annual competition, and there are many classes in this show which are suitable for the amateur. In addition, certain societies which are affiliated to The British Pelargonium and Geranium Society include geranium classes in their summer shows.

Suitable plants. A good geranium judge looks, in the first instance, for a well-grown shapely plant with healthy foliage, and flower heads in the peak of condition. The container itself should be clean and of a suitable size, the plant must be free of dead leaves, virus infection, or chlorosis. The plants should be correctly named, and entered in the right sections.

Preparation. To achieve these requirements, it is essential to start feeding and training the plants early in the year, at least six months before the time of the show. Flower buds should be removed until six weeks before the date of the show. The centre of the plant must be kept open, and growths selected for training should be as low on the main stem as possible. If they are tied to small canes, they will form the main framework of the exhibition plant.

Plants may be shown up to four or five years old, depending on the variety. At one of the British Pelargonium and Geranium Society's shows, Lady Astor showed a magnificent group of scented-leaved varieties which were many years old, but which had been pruned and trained into compact symmetrical bushes. Most ivy-leaved specimens require a cane framework on which to grow.

Trade stands. At some of the Royal Horticultural Society's fortnightly shows in London there are magnificent exhibits of geraniums from several local authorities' parks departments as well as excellent displays from specialist geranium growers. These may be seen at their very best at the annual Chelsea Flower Show.

In 1962 the Southend Parks Department (superintendent, Mr K. McCreadie, N.D.H.) showed one hundred and seventeen varieties, including twenty-five new varieties from America.

These professional displays are well worth a visit from the intending exhibitor. He can learn a great deal from the way in which the plants are staged, and the varieties which are most suitable for exhibition purposes.

Zonals. Single zonal pelargoniums are difficult plants to handle for the show bench. The delicate petals easily drop in transit. The older exhibitors obviate this by putting a small drop of florist's gum in the centre of each floret. Transport of specimen geranium plants for showing is best handled by supporting the side growths with canes, and making a stout paper funnel to enclose the sides of the show plant. Flower trusses may be padded with tissue paper.

The best varieties in this section are Caledonia, a pale purple flower which is extremely floriferous; Dryden, another very free-flowering variety; Skelly's Pride, an unusual salmon variety for exhibition, with uncommon leaves and fringed petals, which do not fall easily; and Willingdon Gem, which has a striking orange flower with a white eye, which will always catch the judge's eye but is difficult to grow as a show plant.

Doubles. The doubles and semi-doubles provide many cultivars which are eminently suitable for exhibition purposes. The dwarf Baronne A. de Rothschild has beautiful cyclamen-coloured flowers with a white eye. The red Dodd's Super Double is one of the largest-flowered geraniums of all, and Dagata is a magnificent pink variety which makes moderate growth and has very large flower trusses. The apple-blossomed Rosebud is another excellent show plant.

Regals. It is among the regals that some of the most handsome exhibition plants may be found. Nearly all the varieties can be grown to show standard by careful cultivation. Caprice, Grand Slam, Grossmama Fischer, Orange Sal, Black Butterfly, and Burgundy are all exceptional varieties.

Regals selected for the show bench can be exhibited in from 5- to 8-inch pots. It is important to shade the plants when they are first repotted, but only for a few days, after which the plants must be moved to full light. The plants must have as much light and air as possible at this stage.

The central stems must be pinched out and plants fed regularly. When the flower buds have formed and are about to open, the plants should then be moved to partial shade so that the actual unfurling of the petals can be controlled. The plants will be at their best when required for show purposes.

Geraniums may be entered in the floral decoration classes, and it is possible from such a wide and unusual range of colours and leaf form to produce some excellent effects. Foliage of the variegated ivy-leaved L'Elégante is very much in demand, as is the pretty foliage of Crispum Variegatum. The foliage of silver-leaved and silver tri-colors are well suited to modern arrangements, and, of course, the very dark reds, purples and blacks to be found among the flowers of the newer regals will give an exotic flavour to any entry in the floral decoration classes.

CHAPTER ELEVEN

List of Species and Varieties

This list of geraniums in cultivation today does not claim to be exhaustive. It does, however, embody many of the new varieties listed by specialist nurserymen and many rediscoveries.

The grouping is that approved by the British Pelargonium and Geranium Society. Where possible colours are given in accordance with the Royal Horticultural Society's Colour Chart. The list of species is by no means complete and is only an indication of what is available in commerce at the time of writing. A very full and complete list of species is given in Derek Clifford's *Pelargoniums*.

F.C.C. = First Class Certificate
A.M. = Award of Merit
H.C. = Highly Commended
R.H.S. = Royal Horticultural Society

ZONAL PELARGONIUMS (*Pelargonium* × *hortorum* Bailey)

1. Mature plants normally more than 8 inches high, grown principally for their flowers and with petals not twisting into a quill.

(a) **Single-flowered group,** having normally no more than five petals.

(i) WHITE

Dorothy Navarro. Large flowers, some pink flush.
Goodwood. Dwarf habit. Cannell, 1907.
Mrs Povey. Free-flowering.
Queen of the Whites (Albion, Avalanche, Claremont, Cresta, Queen of the Belgians, Simplicity, Snowstorm, White Queen). A similar variety, Edward Humphris, gained an A.M., R.H.S., 1953. Very free-flowering, popular variety. Cannell, 1884.
Whitegrove. Buds pale yellow, seedling from Staplegrove Fancy. Parrett, 1960.
White Vesuvius. Pinkish-white, darker zoned leaf than the others.

(ii) PINK

Belvedere Glory (Jules Grèvy). Floriferous, good bedder. Martin (?)

Caledonia (Mrs Sears). Very floriferous, good form. Mallow Purple 630, base of upper petals shaded white. Cannell, 1907.

Caledonian Maiden. Very free-flowering. Rose Opal 022. Caledonian 1953.

Canopus. Large flower, Claret Rose.

Cleopatra (Mrs George Scott, Beckwith's Pride or Beckwith's Pink). Magenta 27/3, medium white eye. Cannell, 1880.

Clere Pink. Salmon-pink.

Constance. Phlox Pink 625.

Coronation. China Rose 024, centred and edged with Turkey Red 721. Caledonian, 1953.

Countess of Jersey (Joan Fontaine, Derwent Pride). Free-flowering. Dawn Pink 523/2, veined darker, small white eye. Cannell, 1911.

C. W. Ward (Mrs Ward, Dot Slade). Large flower, Camellia Rose 622, veined darker, small white eye. Lemoine, 1898.

Delight (Hamelin). Large flower. Vermilion 18/1.

Eden Perfection. White, veined Porcelain Rose 620, blotched Azalea Pink 618. Parrett, 1959. H.C., R.H.S., 1960.

Eva (Hamlet, Jessie C. Dick, J. C. Dick). Dwarf variety, large flower, blend of Signal Red 19/3 and Crimson 22.

French Bouquet. Camellia Rose 622/3.

Harriet Le Hair. Salmon Pink.

Harry Butler. Small flowers, good bedder. Fuchsine Pink 627 and Signal Red 7/9 at base. Butler of Teddington, 1959. A.M., R.H.S. Trials, 1960.

Hidcote. Fuchsine Pink 627, veined darker.

Highland Queen. Large blooms, pale Tyrian Purple, white centre. Telston, 1950.

Iris. Rose Opal 022. Pearson, 1898.

J. F. Donning. Large flowers, Geranium Rose.

John Cross. Large flower, strong grower. Crimson 22/2, veined and shot Carmine 21/1. Telston, 1950.

Kennard Castle. Camellia Rose 622/1.

Lady Folkestone. Large flowers, free-flowering. Fuchsine Pink 627/2, white base to upper petals. Cannell, 1907.

L. E. Wharton. Camellia Rose 622/1, large white eye.

Millfield Rival (Rosamund). Strong-growing plant, large flower, large white eye. Tyrian Rose 24 /1.

Mrs David Alston. Geranium Lake 20/2, veined.

Mrs E. G. Hill. Carmine Rose 62/1, darker veins in upper petals, blotched Begonia 619 at base of petals. Good bedder. Bruant, 1889. H.C., R.H.S. Trials, 1960.

Mrs Gill. Phlox Pink, paling to centre.

Mrs Norman Burden. Pale Rose Opal. Telston, 1950?

Nanette. Large shapely flowers. Geranium Lake 20/1, shaded Rose Madder 20/3, large white eye. Clifton, 1902?

Nottinghill Beauty (Bartleman, Brighton Gem). Good bedder, Geranium Lake 20.

Orvieto. Rhodamine Pink. Telston, 1960.

Oystershell. Very pale pink flowers. Telston, 1956.

Patience. Rose Pink. Telston, 1960.

Pink Crampel. Neyron Rose 623, veined and flushed with red.

Pride of the West (Dublin, Olive Baker.) Very large flowers of fine form. Crimson 22/1, flushed scarlet, small white eye.

Princess Anne (Prince Charles, Christine). Fuchsine Pink 627, white eye. Cross, 1952, a reintroduction of an old variety.

Prince Philip. White flushed with rose-pink.

Rose Queen. Rose Madder 23, shot with pink, base of upper petals white. Cannell, 1916.

Satin Bow. Pale Tyrian Rose.

Sir Philip Sidney. Pale Persian Rose, very large blooms, large white eye, Persian Rose 6 28/2. Telston, 1880?

Tiger (Lady Emily). Fuchsine Pink 627, large white eye. Pearson, 1872.

Vesna. Carmine Rose. Telston, 1958, from Czechoslovakia.

(iii) RED

Aileene. Empire Rose brushed carmine.

Aldenham. Large flowers, Currant Red 821/2, shaded Cardinal Red 822/1, small white eye. Cannell, 1907.

Amaranth. Geranium Lake.

Beatrix Little. Dwarf habit, large flowers, Vermilion 18. Sport from King of Denmark. Little, 1950.

Biddie. Bedding variety, bright Vermilion. Telson.

Charles Blair. Large habit, Cherry 722.

Copper Kettle. Very floriferous. Signal Red. 1950?

Cymric. Very large flowers. Signal Red 719, upper petals, lower petals Blood Red 820, shot with Turkey Red 721.

Darenth. Small flowers, dark crimson. Telston, 1950.

David Blake. Small flowers. Turkey Red 721.

Doris Moore. Very free-flowering, good bedder. Cherry 722/1. Clifton, 1938.

Drummer Boy (Banbury Cross, Countess of Birkenhead, Jupiter, Mars). Large flowers. Dutch Vermilion 717, small white eye. Case of Taunton. (Countess of Birkenhead, Thorpe, 1952, has a slight difference in eye.)

Dryden (Santa Monica, Lady Dryden). Flowers in winter. Very free-flowering, large truss. Geranium Lake 20/1 on upper petals, lower petals shaded darker, large white eye. Pearson, 1895.

Eden Beauty. Very large flowers. Crimson Magenta. Parrett, 1950?

Eden Roc. Large flowers, good bedder, short jointed, Dutch Vermilion 717. Parrett, 1959. H.C., R.H.S. Trials, 1960.

Elizabeth Cartwright. Difficult grower, large flower. Cherry 722/1, upper petals shaded Dutch Vermilion 717. Humphris, 1949, A.M., R.H.S., 1950. Sander Medal, 1951.

Feuerriese. Turkey Red. Telston, 1960, from Switzerland.

Grenadier (Alice de Vincennes, Lady Alice of Valencia, Mrs William Oliver, Mary Seton). Dutch Vermilion 717, lighter in the upper petals, large white eye.

Hadrian. Good bedder. Geranium Lake 20, upper petals, lower scarlet 19, dark zone in leaf. Parrett, 1961.

Harvest Moon. Free-flowering. Poppy red, white base to upper petals.

Henry Jacoby (Lansbury, Thomas Earle). Dwarf habit, free-flowering. Upper petals Orient Red 819/1, lower petals Turkey Red 721 and Cherry 722. Pearson, 1880. F.C.C., R.H.S., 1897.

Hilda Rawlings. Large flowers, good bedder. Orient Red 819. Rawlings of Banbury, 1959. A.M., R.H.S. Trials, 1960.

Hope. Very large flowers. Turkey Red 721, upper petals shaded Tyrian Purple, large white eye.

Ian. Scarlet, white eye. Telston, 1950?

J. M. Barrie. Geranium Lake 20/1.

Kingswood. Large flowers, Fuchsia Purple 28/2 and Signal Red 719. Large white eye. Cannell, 1907.

Lady Harold Smith. Good bedder. Signal Red 719. Thorpe, 1950. A.M., R.H.S. Trials, 1960.

Lawrence Johnstone. Small flowers. Currant Red 821/1.

Lilian Duff. Large flowers. Orient Red 819.

Meteor. Large flowers. Orange-red. Telston, 1960, from Czechoslovakia.

Mirabelle. Zoneless leaf, Signal Red.

Mrs Eddowes (Sir Thomas Hanbury, Captain Holford, Leonidas, Petunia). Very large flowers. Tyrian Purple 727, shaded Poppy Red 16, with Signal Red 719 on upper petals, and small white eye.

My Fair Lady. Claret Rose, white eye.

Olinger. Signal Red.

Pandora, Geranium Lake 20.

Paul Crampel. Well-known bedding variety. Vermilion 18. Lemoine, 1892.

Penda. Good bedder. Orient Red, white eye brushed purple. Parrett, 1960.

Poet's Pride. Claret Rose, white eye.

President McKinley. Rose Bengal, shaded Spiraea Red.

Rosemary. Very large flower, Mandarin Red. Parrett, 1960.

Ruby. Small flowers, Orient Red 819/3. White base to upper petals, veined Tyrian Purple. Caledonian, 1950.

Scatterbrain. Small flowers. Rose Red 724, large white eye. A reintroduction by Caledonian, 1952.

Sensation. Large flowers. Turkey Red 721, small white eye.

Thames. Scarlet, white eye.

Stansted. Pillarbox Red, white base to upper petals. Parrett, 1957. Sport from Staplegrove Fancy.

The Sirdar. Strong grower, rich Crimson.

The Stag. Tyrian Rose, carmine shading on upper petals.

Vendetta. Crimson.

Victorious. Very large plant with large flowers. Dutch Vermilion 717, shaded darker. Clifton, 1903?

(iv) SALMON

Barbara Hope (Phyllis, Willingdon Beauty, Roedale Glory, Duchess of Portland). Carmine 21/3, veined lighter, small white eye. Pearson, 1899.

Betty Catchpole. Small flowers. Signal Red 719/3. Catchpole, 1950.

Cardiff. Small flowers. Camellia Rose 622, darker at the edges.

Clarence Elliot. Curled petals. Salmon, paler markings.

Deep Skelly's. Similar to Skelly's Pride. Poppy Red 16. Caledonian, 1957. Sport of Skelly's Pride.

Edward Hockey (Afterglow). Dwarf habit, large flowers. Geranium Lake 20/2, flushed Vermilion 18/1, dark veins in upper petals, small white eye.

Elizabeth Angus. Large flowers, Porcelain Rose 620, flushed Tyrian Rose, creamy-white eye. Ayton, 1955.

Estrelita. Salmon with orange shading.

Gwendolin Lysley. Camellia Rose 622/1 base and centre, Begonia 619.

Honeymoon. Dwarf grower, white flower, shaded and veined to centre. Porcelain Rose 620.

Lady of Spain. Large flowers. Camellia Rose 621/1, veined darker, large white eye. Schmidt, 1947.

Lisbeth. Rich salmon. Telston, 1950.

Mrs Cannell. Dwarf habit, free-flowering. Camellia Rose 622/1, shaded Mandarin Red 17/1. Cannell, 1898.

Murray Horne. Empire Rose.

Ostmark. Large flowers. Porcelain Rose. Telston, 1960, from Czechoslovakia.

Peach. Small grower. Peach Pink.

Porta Maris. Good bedder, small flowers. Mandarin Red 17. Margate Parks, 1932. Cross between Maxim Kovalevski and Nottinghill Beauty.

Salmon Crampel. Large flowers. Good bedder. Bold zone in leaf. Claret Rose 021/1.

Salmon Kovalevski (Susan Baldwin). Dwarfish habit. Camellia Rose 622/2, faint veins. Telston, 1952, as Susan Baldwin; A.M., 1954, as Salmon Kovalevski.

Skelly's Pride (Flame, Salmon Fringed, Jeanne). Strong habit, glabrous leaves. Dutch Vermilion 717/1, petals crenate.

Sunset. Salmon, with orange shades.

The Boar (Salmonia). Often confused with *P. salmoneum*. Single, primitive salmon flowers, straggly growth, heavily zoned leaves. A.M., R.H.S., 1955, as *P. salmoneum*!

Victory. Small flowers. Porcelain Rose 620.

Willingdon Beauty. Large flowers. Geranium Lake 20. Clifton, 1930.

Zeebrugge (Sunrise, Le Mousseau, Ideal). Dwarf plant, large truss. Camellia Rose 622, veined and shaded Geranium Lake 20. Lemoine, 1902, as Ideal.

(v) ORANGE

Aurore (Heather Bell). Dwarf habit. Mandarin Red 17/1, upper petals based Scarlet 19/2. Lemoine, 1896.

Campbell's Comet. Bright orange, a shade deeper than Kovalevski.

Flambeau. Large flower. Signal Red 719/3.

George Coates. Mandarin Red 17, mottled white eye. Very similar to Willingdon Gem.

Golden Lion (Cuba). Azalea Pink 618, shot with Mandarin Red 17/1. Cannell, 1916.

Janet Scott. Large flowers. Dutch Vermilion 717.

Maxim Kovalevski (Maxime-Maxine-Kovalevsky, Diablo, Juliana, Santa Barbara, J. H. Laurens). Dutch Vermilion 717/2. A.M., R.H.S., 1911. Lemoine, 1906.

Oranje Gem. Orange 12, medium white eye. Parrett, 1960.
Sansovino. Dutch Vermilion 717/1.
Willingdon Gem (Nouvelle Aurore). Large flowers. Dutch Vermilion 717/3. Large white eye. Clifton, 1920. Lemoine, 1920, as Nouvelle Aurore. Cert. of Merit, Paris, 1923.

(vi) MAGENTA

George Burgwin (Mary Jane). Small thin-petalled flowers. Magenta 27, white shading on upper petals.
Harlow Pearl. Strong grower, large flower, good form. White, pearly sheen with the faintest suggestion of magenta. Cross, 1958. Seedling Caledonia × Queen of the Whites.
Lilac Delight. Free-flowering. Phlox Purple 632/1, veined darker. Caledonian, 1956.
Lord Curzon (Winston Churchill). Vigorous grower. Tyrian Purple 727, large white eye. Cannell, 1900, as Winston Churchill.
Maid of Perth. Large flowers. Cyclamen Purple 30/1, white base to upper petal. Telston, 1956.
Meg. Rose Madder. Telston, 1960.
Norah Docker. Free-flowering. Fuchsia Purple 28, base of upper petals scarlet. Caledonian, 1957. Very close to Stirling Stent.
Primula. Rhodamine Pink 727, white base to upper petals, edged Fuchsine Pink 627. Parrett, 1956.
Prince of Wales (Rudyard Kipling, Anne Elizabeth). Free flowering. Tyrian Purple 727/1, upper petals shaded Signal Red 719. Pearson, 1890, as Rudyard Kipling.
Rene. Persian Rose.
Stirling Stent (A. H. Thomas). Poor grower, small flower. Solferino Purple 26, shaded Rose Bengal 25, small white eye.
Titania. Magenta 27.
Vera Dillon. Dwarf habit, free-flowering. Magenta 27, upper part shaded Signal Red 719. Dillon, 1948.
Victor Hugo. Pale magenta. Lemoine.
Wembley Gem. Floriferous. Magenta, small white eye.

(vii) PICOTEE AND FANCY

Carmel. Very free-flowering, white petals edged with Cherry 722/2. Schmidt, 1947.
Ecstasy. Large flower, white marked and veined with Tyrian Rose 24/3. U.S.A.?

63

Edelweiss. White with irregularly marked pink margin. Lemoine, 1912.

Flowerfield. Tall grower, white flower spotted and edged Rose Madder 23. Ayton, 1950.

Isabel Pearce. White, edged and speckled Signal Red 719. Parrett, 1958.

Lady Sarah Wilson. Dwarf form of Staplegrove Fancy. Cannell, 1900.

Lady Warwick. Very free-flowering, white petals sharply edged with Magenta 27. Cannell, 1900.

Mauretania (Daintiness). Very free-flowering, white flower with inner ring of Camellia Rose 622. Cannell, 1900.

Miriam Basey. Rose Madder, white edge.

Mr Wren. Dark red, ringed at the edge with pure white. Recent introduction from U.S.A.

New Life (L'Avenir). Large flower, petals striped from centre to edge with white. Henderson, 1869. Sport from Vesuvius.

Pink Skelly's (Sweet William, Madame Thibault). Sport of Skelly's Pride. Crenate petals. White shaded to Persian Rose 628/3, veined lighter.

Spotted Gem (Purpurea). Strong grower, white petals, flushed Mallow Purple 630 on upper petals, lower petals spotted Rhodamine Purple. Parker, 1890.

Staplegrove Fancy. Large flowers. White, clouded and spotted with Carmine 21 and 21/1. Case of Taunton, 1905.

Warley. White flowers, veined and edged with Geranium Lake 20. Cannell, 1900.

White Bird's Egg (Skylark). Free-flowering, small flowers, white spotted and tinted Roseine Purple.

Xenia Field. Small flower. Pale Carmine Rose, white veins shading to Scarlet 19 at centre. Telston, 1953.

(b) Double and semi-double-flowered group

All varieties which normally have more than five petals to a flower, except those which are described under the rosebud, cactus-flowered, fancy-leaved and miniature sections.

(i) WHITE

Abbey White. Good bedder. Chalk white.

Baron de Layres. More compact than Hermine.

Hermine (Hermione, Heroine, Gertrude Ashworth, Blanche Berard, Fratelli Ferrari). Vigorous habit, small flowers. Slightly pink outdoors. Rozaine, 1894. As Gertrude Ashworth received A.M., R.H.S., 1900.

Regal pelargonium: Burgundy,
very deep red, nearly black flowers

Regal pelargonium: Rhodamine, purple
with a white centre

Regal
pelargonium:
Valencia, this
specimen had
over 200 flower
trusses

L'Elégante,
an ivy-leaved
pelargonium,
the edges of
whose leaves
turn pink if
the plant is
kept on the
dry side

Fragrans, a
scented–leaved
variety

Madame Recamier. Medium flowers, dark foliage, greenish buds Lemoine, 1904.

Ryecroft. White. Large flowers. Jones of Lewisham, 1890.

(ii) PINK

Anais Segalis (Gillian Clifford). Free-flowering, large trusses. Spiraea Red 025/2, centre flushed with Rose Opal 022. Lemoine, 1893. Caledonian, 1953, Seedling Victory × Hermine.

Audrey (Pasteur). S. D. Rose Bengal 25/3, centre paler.

Baronne A. de Rothschild. Dwarf, large semi-double flowers. Phlox Pink 621/3 on 621/2, large white eye. Bruant.

Bournewater. Carnation Pink.

Cal. Good bedder. Soft pink. Dave Adgate, Ohio, U.S.A., 1955. An 'Irene' variety.

Dagata. Large flowers, semi-double. Strong grower. Magenta 27/2, shaded darker, large white eye.

Delicata. Pale Carmine Rose, lighter edges.

Duchess. Dwarf grower. Phlox Pink 625/1.

Emma Vossels. Free-flowering. Dwarf growth. Pale pink.

Fleur de Rose (Queen Alexandra), Large flowers, semi-double. Fuchsia Purple, 628/2, white eye. Bruant, 1901.

Garibaldi. Vigorous grower. White, veined and spotted Carmine 21/2. Ayton, 1955.

Genetrex. Semi-double very open flowers. Lower petals Crimson 22/1, upper petals Geranium Lake 20/1. Small white base to lower petals.

Hugo de Vries. Free-flowering. Porcelain Rose 620. Bruant, 1902.

Irene. Good bedder, bright red. Dave Adgate, Ohio, U.S.A., 1955.

Janetta. White, lightly flushed Camellia Rose.

Jean Oberle (Buxton). Strong grower, large truss. Pink. Bruant, 1908.

Jewel (Lord Derby, Constance and H. M. Stanley). Small flowers, tight truss. Rose Madder 23/1, white eye.

Lady Ilchester. Mallow Purple 630/2.

Madame Roscleur (Madame de la Fourcould). Small flowers. Phlox Pink, white eye.

Mauve Queen. Dwarf habit, large flowers, semi-double. White shot with Phlox Pink 625/1.

Memories. Free-flowering, semi-double. Fuchsia Purple 28/3, upper petals white based. U.S.A.

Mrs Lawrence (Lady Ellendon). Dwarf habit, small flower, good bedder. Rose Pink 427.

E   65

Nancy Lindsey. Neyron Rose 623.

Nydia. Dwarf, small flowers. White centred Rhodonite Red 0022. Miller, Great Britain, 1898.

Olympia (Madame Hoste, Madame Hoist). Large flower, semi-double. Fuchsine Pink 627/1.

Penny. Neon Pink, semi-double. Long flowering season. Dave Adgate, Ohio, U.S.A., 1955. An Irene type.

Phenomenal. Strong grower, large semi-double. Fuchsine Pink 627.

Pink Raspail. Free-flowering, small truss. Upper petals based white suffused Persian Rose 628/1. Cannell, 1900.

Promenade. Neyron Rose.

Radia. Delft Rose.

R. A. Turner (Apple Blossom). Dwarf habit, large open semi-double flowers. Cyclamen Purple 30, large white eye. Cannell, 1880.

Schwarzwalderin. Compact grower. Free-flowering. Claret Rose. Telston, 1958; introduction from Switzerland.

Senegalis. Carmine Rose.

Thomas Binnie. Camellia Rose.

Trautlieb. Dwarf habit. Good bedder. Telston, 1959. Introduction from Switzerland.

(iii) RED

Astrakan. Dwarf growth. Small flowers. Turkey Red 721, shaded crimson. Lemoine, 1912.

Brilliant. Dwarf habit. Large flowers, semi-double. Vermilion 18.

Brussels. Turkey Red.

Buccleugh Gem. Large habit. Large flowers. Carmine Rose 621.

Captain Flayelle (Captain Hazel). Strong grower, large semi-double flower. Signal Red 719.

Captain Jolivet. Tyrian Rose 24, purple in lower petals. Bruant, 1897.

Charentin. Dwarf grower, small flower. Dark Red.

Chavarri Hermanos. Large flowers, semi-double. Dutch Vermilion 717. Bruant, 1907, from Spain.

Cherison. Dutch Vermilion 717.

Colonel Drabbe. Large flowers. Turkey Red 721, white eye.

Decorator (Red Denmark, President Baillet, Alphonse Ricard). Strong grower, large semi-double flowers. Dutch Vermilion 717. Bruant, 1900.

Dodd's Super Double. Very large habit, probably the largest of all zonal geraniums. Very double flowers, Carmine 21. Dodd discovered, reintroduced Caledonian, 1954.

Double Jacoby (Sainte Honoré). Dwarf habit, small flowers. Orient Red 819. Turkey Red 721. Cannell, 1896.

Dutch Double Scarlet. Turkey Red.

Edmund Lachenal. Orient Red. Lachenal was a Swiss botanist.

Electric Pink. Strong grower, shades of Tyrian Rose 727, Rose Red 724, Tyrian Rose 24. Caledonian, 1955. A reintroduction.

Flamme Poitevene. Geranium Lake. Bruant, 1890.

F. V. Raspail. Dwarf grower, small flowers. Dutch Vermilion 717. Lemoine, 1878.

Gustav Emich (Lord Kitchener, Kitchener of Khartoum, K. of K). Free-flowering. Good bedder. Scarlet 19. Lemoine/Cannell, 1898. Pearson, as Lord Kitchener. A.M., R.H.S., 1949. A.M., R.H.S. Trials, 1960.

Hall Caine. Bright red, white eye.

Herzog Wilhelm. Signal Red. Telston, 1958. Introduction from Switzerland.

Irvington Beauty (American Beauty). Strong grower, large flowers. Rose Madder 23, shot Carmine 22. U.S.A.

Isobel Turner. Large flowers. Carmine 21, shaded Rose Madder 23.

Josephine. Dwarf habit, small flower. Signal Red 719/1.

King of the Belgians. Good bloomer. Bright scarlet.

Le Colosse. Large habit, large flowers. Orient Red 819.

Margaret de Pynion (Marguerite de Pinon). Dwarf grower, small flowers. Persian Red. Bruant, 1893.

Miss Perkins. Large grower, large flower. Rose Bengal 25, veined Geranium Lake 20. Cannell, 1910.

Paul Reboux. Cherry Red. Telston, 1958. Introduction from France.

Radiance. Scarlet.

Rainbow. Dwarf grower, small flowers. Turkey Red 721, veined Rose Bengal 25/1. Miller, Great Britain, 1895.

Roscobie (Hornsey Crimson). Dwarf grower, small flowers. Rose Madder 23, shaded Crimson 22.

Rubin. Dwarf grower, good bedding variety. Rose-red. Telston, 1958. Reintroduction from Switzerland.

Ryecroft Pride. Small flowers. Cherry Red 722, Signal Red 719, marked with Tyrian Purple. Jones of Lewisham, 1890.

Triomphe de Nancy. Large truss. Rose Madder 23/1, veined darker. Gerbeaux, 1894.

Turtle's Surprise. Dwarf grower, white stem, small flowers. Dutch Vermilion 717. Cannell, 1890. A.M., 1890.

Ulmer Brilliant. Dutch Vermilion 717. Telston, 1958. Introduction from Switzerland.

Pelargoniums for all Purposes

(iv) SALMON

Dr M. Tyrs. Small flowers. Geranium Lake. Telston, 1960. Introduction from Czechoslovakia.

Flesh Pink. Strong grower, small flowers. White base, flushed French Rose 520/2, lighter towards margins.

Genevieve. Strong grower. Signal Red 719/3, lightening, edged with Jasper Red 018. Ayton, 1955.

Irma. Sparse truss. Leaves glabrous. Begonia 619, lower petals Porcelain Rose 620/1. Large white centre. California, 1939.

King of Denmark (Beauté Poitevine, Slitrig Gem, Countess, Progress). Strong grower, very free-flowering, popular bedding plant. Geranium Lake 20/2 with Crimson 22/2 veins. Cannell, 1887. Bruant, 1877, as Beauté Poitevine.

Lullaby. Dwarf grower, floriferous. Porcelain Rose 620. Outer petals blotched Neyron Rose 623/2. Miller, California, 1941.

Madame Charlotte (Madame Charotte). Strong grower, large flowers. Claret Rose 021, paling and veined with Rose Opal 022/1. Gerbeaux, 1892.

Medway. Carmine-rose.

Queen of Denmark (Mme Landry, Charles Richet). Strong grower. Porcelain Rose 620 with Rose Madder 23/2. 1907?

The Speaker (Casimir Perier). Strong grower. Large flowers. Rose Madder 23/1 marked Carmine 21/1. Cannell, 1912.

(v) ORANGE

Lave (Springfield Orange, Prince of Orange). Dwarf plant, medium flowers. Dutch Vermilion 717/1. Bruant, 1902.

Orangesonne. Good bedder. Orange. Telston, 1960. Introduction from Switzerland.

Profusion (Sunbeam). Dwarf habit. Capsicum Red 716/3.

(vi) MAGENTA

A. M. Mayne (A. Maynis, A. Magne, Springfield Violet). Strong grower, large flower. Tyrian Purple 727, shaded Dutch Vermilion 717. Bruant, 1913.

Avon. Solferino Purple. Telston, 1958.

Blue Fox (Renard Bleu). Floriferous. Blue-purple. Telston, 1960. Introduction from Czechoslovakia.

Festiva Maxima. Strong grower. No zone on leaf. Tyrian Purple 727. This is very close to A. M. Mayne.

List of Species and Varieties

Glorious (Old Port). Dwarf grower. Semi-double. Tyrian Purple 727/1; shot with darker purple.

Le Lutin. Dwarf grower. Tyrian Purple 727/2, shot with red. Lemoine, 1907.

Monsieur Emil David. Strong grower. Large flowers, semi-double. Magenta 27, large white eye. Bruant, 1906.

Mrs A. Freer. Dwarf grower. Small flowers. Tyrian Purple 727, some scarlet.

Mrs Chaplin (Commines, Pegasa). Large flowers, white eye. Magenta 27, with red shading. Gerbeaux, 1912.

Niobe. Solferino Purple with scarlet eye.

Paul Humphris. Tyrian Purple shaded crimson.

Royal Purple (Brook's Purple, Pickled Cabbage, Frogmore, William Tell, Mrs Rees Mogg, Hornsey Violet, Gwendy, Old King Cole). Good grower. Tyrian Purple, 727/3. Cannell, 1896.

(vii) PICOTEE AND FANCY

Charles Gounoud (Madame Fuiner, Charles Fuinier, Madame Guineau). Vigorous grower. Large flowers. White based, shaded and shot with Magenta 27. Gerbeaux, 1897.

Double New Life (York and Lancaster, Flag of Denmark, Stars and Stripes, Peppermint Stick). Dwarf plant, small flowers. Vermilion 18, alternate petals, Porcelain Rose 620/3, crenate petals. Smith, 1879.

Double Pink Bird's Egg. Semi-double. Good grower, light purple, flecked and marked darker. Bruant, 1908.

E. Herbert. Strong grower, large flowers. Semi-double. Flushed and marked Phlox Pink, darker centre of Neyron Rose and scarlet.

Emperor Nicholas. Dwarf grower. Floriferous. White speckled Phlox Pink, darker to edge of petals.

Fraicheur (Canadian Pink and White). Strong grower. Large flower, edged with and speckled pink. Bruant, 1884. (A common French name for several varieties.)

Margery Boyd (Paton Pink). Pink, spotted darker. Mrs Boyd. Re-discovered in Australia, French origin?

Mlle Gauthier. Dwarf grower. Pale pink, spotted darker. Gerbeaux, 1900.

Mrs Tarrant. Dwarf habit. Good bedder. Small leaves. White edged and shaded Neyron Rose 23.

Robella. Strong grower, large flower. Camellia Rose 622, marked as Charles Gounoud.

Trésor. Poor grower, small flowers. Flowers white striped and flaked with Porcelain Rose. Gerbeaux, 1895.

(c) **Rosebud group**

Fully double and 'hearted', the middle petals remaining unopened like the bud of a rose.

Apple Blossom Rosebud. Strong grower, large truss. White, edged Porcelain Rose 628, some green in centre. Canada?

Pink Rambler (Rose Rambler). Similar to Red Rambler but flowers pink.

Red Rambler. Medium grower. Geranium Lake 20, underside of petals 20/2.

Rosebud (Plum Rambler). Similar to Red Rambler but Tyrian Purple flowers.

Rosebud Supreme (Red Rosebud Scarlet Rambler). Similar to Red Rambler but darker.

Snow King (Schneekonig). White flowers. Telston, 1960. Introduction from Czechoslovakia.

2. Mature plants more than 8 inches high and grown for their flowers, having petals twisted into a quill.

(d) **Cactus flowered Group, single and double**

(i) WHITE

Noel. Double flowers. White. Schmidt, 1948.

Snow Queen. Single, small flowers. White. Cannell, 1900.

(ii) PINK

Attraction. Long, double, feathery petals. Camellia Rose 622/2, veined darker.

Fascination. Single flowers. Turkey Red 721/1, shaded lighter. Bunn. A.M., R.H.S., 1923.

H. Greenhill. Double flowers. Tyrian Rose 24/3. Cannell, 1900.

Ida Morland. Double flowers. Rose Opal 022/2.

Mrs Salter Bevis (Beves). Double, small flowers. Pale magenta and white.

(iii) SALMON

Corallina. Dwarf grower. Porcelain Rose 620.

Coronia. Dwarf grower. Long petals. Camellia Rose 222.

Morning Star. Strong grower. Orange Red. Schmidt, 1953.

Southern Cross. Strong grower. Large flowers. Salmon Coral. Schmidt, 1953.

(iv) ORANGE

Tangerine. Dwarf grower. Double flower. Dutch Vermilion 717/3.

(v) RED

Alfred Zitzer. Large flowers. Double. Rose Red 724/1 shaded Cherry 722.
Brockbury Scarlet. Single flowers. Signal Red 719/1.
Chinese Dragon. Sport from Fire Dragon. Petals less furled. Signal Red 719. Caledonian, 1954.
Fire Dragon. Small double flowers. Signal Red 719. Cannell, 1900. Sport of F. V. Raspail.

3. Mature plants normally more than 8 inches high, grown principally for their foliage, single and double-flowered.

(e) Fancy-leaved group

(i) SILVER-LEAVED

Caroline Schmidt (Wilhelm Languth, Deutscher Seiger). Good bedder. Flower double. Geranium Lake 20. Leaf Lavender Green 000761. border Straw Yellow 604/3. Germany, 1890?
Chelsea Gem (Mrs Churchill, Lady Randolph Churchill). Dwarf grower. Flower small. Double. Phlox Pink 625/2, white eye. Bull, 1880.
Flower of Spring (Kathleen Harrop). Single flower. Dutch Vermilion 717. Leaf Lavender Green 000761, edged with Dresden Yellow 64/3. Turner, 1860. F.C.C., R.H.S., 1862.
Foster's Seedling (Mary Anderson, Mountains of Snow, Hills of Snow). Single flower. Rose Madder. Cannell, 1900.
Little Trot (Mrs Newton). Very small single flowers. Reversion of Madame Salleron. Carmine Rose 621. Post, 1896.
Mrs J. C. Mappin (Mrs Mapping). Single flowers. Growth strong. Flower white, flushed Porcelain Rose 620/3, upper petals Porcelain Rose 620. Leaf similar to Flower of Spring. Townshend, 1880.
Mrs Parker. Double flowers, small. Flower, Phlox Pink 625. Leaf as Caroline Schmidt. Parker, 1880. A.M., R.H.S., 1960.
S. A. Nutt. Single flowers. Flower Turkey Red. Leaf Lavender Green, silver edge. Telston, 1960, from U.S.A.

71

(ii) SILVER TRICOLORS

Dolly Varden. Dwarf grower. Small single flower. Flower Signal Red 719. Leaf green, white-edged, purple zone marked with carmine. Morris, 1880, H.C., R.H.S., 1890.

Eva Fish. Single flower. Flower red. Leaf cream-white and Lake Rose zone. Cannell, 1880.

Lass o' Gowrie (Carse o' Gowrie). Single flowers. Dwarf grower. Flower Vermilion 18. Leaf, outer border Primrose Yellow 601/3, shadow zone Porcelain Rose 620, centre Willow Green 000862, zoned Purple Madder. Henderson 1860. F.C.C., R.H.S., 1868.

Miss Burdett Coutts. Dwarf grower, very slow. Single flower. Flower Dutch Vermilion 717. Leaf like Lass o' Gowrie but much brighter scarlet splashes. Henderson, 1860. Grieve, 1867.

Miss Farren. Similar to Dolly Varden but stronger growing. Cannell, before 1882.

(iii) GOLDEN LEAVED

Beth Watts. Leaf pale gold. Flower single, pale Porcelain Rose.

Cloth of Gold. Single flower. Flower Vermilion 717. Leaf Yellow-green.

Creed's Seedling (Golden Crampel Dwarf Gold Leaf). Flower single, Vermilion. Leaf Citron Green 763 to Lettuce Green 861/2. Reversion of Crystal Palace Gem.

Golden Crest. Round frilly leaf. Flower rose-pink. Parrett, 1959.

Golden Orfe. Large flower for type. Flower salmon-pink, cream reverse. Leaf gold. Campbell. 1960.

Robert Fish. Dwarf habit, small flowers. Vermilion. Turner, 1871.

Verona (Pink Cloth of Gold). Small single flowers. Flower Phlox Pink 625/1, Leaf Citron Green 763 to Lettuce Green 861/2. Cannell, 1900. H.C., R.H.S. Trials, 1960.

(iv) BRONZE AND GOLD

Adam's Quilt. Single flowers. Flower Rose Pink. Leaf Bronze zone. Ayton, 1963.

Beauty of Calderdale. Single flowers. Flower Geranium Lake. Leaf Pod Green, Chocolate zone. Before 1880. Mentioned by Grieve.

Beauty of Hebron. Single flower. Flower Porcelain Rose, white eye. Leaf Bronze zone.

Black Douglas. Strong grower, small flower. Flower Vermilion. Cannell, 1880.

Bronze Corinne. Double flower. Flower scarlet. Leaf Bronze zone. Cannell, 1910.

Madame Nonin, an
older Unique type

Rollinson's Unique,
one of the Unique
type

Catford Belle, an
Angel pelargonium, with
purple petals

P. *tetragonum*, a
South African species

The Boar,
with dark green
leaves and salmon
flowers

P. tomentosum, the peppermint-scented
pelargonium

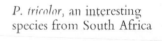

P. tricolor, an interesting
species from South Africa

P. triste, the Sad
Geranium, with carrot-like
leaves

Pelargonium leaves
differ widely in shape and
colour as can be seen
below, left to right:

Top row: Mrs Pollock, Red
Black Vesuvius, Maréchal
MacMahon, Verona

Centre row: Mrs Quilter,
Golden Harry Hieover,
L'Elégante, Lass o' Gowrie,
Crystal Palace Gem

Bottom row: Lady Plymouth,
Flower of Spring, Happy
Thought, Mr Henry Cox

Bronze Queen. Single flower. Flower Signal Red. Leaf pale green, Bronze zone. Cannell, 1910.

Golden Fleece. Single flowers. Flowers Porcelain Rose.

Harrison's Weir. Single flower larger than Mrs Quilter. Flower Porcelain Rose. Leaf pale green, Chestnut zone. Grieve, 1860.

His Majesty. Single flower. Flower Vermilion. Leaf Pod Green, Bronze zone.

Italia Unita. Leaf green, Bronze zone. Flower double, orange-red. Grieve, 1870.

Magenta MacMahon. Leaf as Maréchal MacMahon. Flower single Magenta.

Maréchal MacMahon (The Czar, King George V, Jubilee). Dwarf habit, small single flower. Flower Dutch Vermilion 717. Leaf broad zone nearly to outer edge, Garnet Brown 00918/3, inner colour Citron Green 763 to Lettuce Green 861/3. Cannell, 1880. F.C.C., R.H.S., 1872 and 1897.

Masterpiece. Dwarf grower, small double flower. Flower Rose Opal 022, shaded Camellia Rose 622. Leaf as Mrs Quilter. Cannell, 1897.

Mrs Quilter. Dwarf growth, small single flower. Flower Begonia 619/2 shading to 619. Leaf similar to MacMahon but narrower and lighter. Laing, 1880.

(v) BLACK-LEAVED

(Leaves black, purple-black or dark zoned)

Distinction (One in a Ring). Dwarf habit, single flower. Flower Cherry 722/1. Leaf dentate, Spinach Green 0960, narrow clear black zone. Henderson, 1880?

(vi) BUTTERFLY-LEAVED

(With Butterfly marking of distinct tone or hue in centre of leaf)

Black Cox. Dwarf grower, single flower. Flower Empire Rose 0621/1 shaded darker. Leaf very dark green with broad black zone, shows lighter butterfly mark. Caledonian, 1955. Sport from Mr Henry Cox.

Crampel's Master. Strong grower, large single flower. Flower Vermilion 7. Leaf mid-green, lighter butterfly mark.

Crystal Palace Gem. Single flower, dwarf grower. Flower Cherry Red 722. Leaf Citron Green 763 with butterfly mark, Spinach Green 0960. Henderson, 1869.

Freak of Nature. Dwarf grower, very slow, small, single flower. Flower Vermilion. Leaf Pod Green, very large cream mark in centre. Gray, 1880.

Happy Thought. Medium grower, single flower. Flower Cherry Red 722. Leaf Spinach Green 0960, butterfly mark Citron Green 763. Grieve, before 1868. H.C., R.H.S., 1960. Lynes, 1877.

Lady Luck. Flower red. Leaf Pod Green, cream butterfly mark. Translucent stems. Telston, 1960. Introduction from U.S.A.

Mangle's Variegated (Manglesi). Semi-prostrate growth. Flower garnet scarlet. Leaf, dark green butterfly on lettuce green background.

Mrs G. Clark. Double flower. Flower pale pink. Leaf pale green, cream butterfly mark, white stem.

Pink Happy Thought. Similar to Happy Thought, but with bright pink flower. Telston, 1959. Introduction from U.S.A.

(vii) GOLDEN TRICOLORS

Jane Maxwell. Flower orange-red. Leaf, bronze and red zone with yellow edge. This is probably a hybrid Ivy-Leaf. Telston, 1960. Introduction from U.S.A.

Lady Cullum. Small single flower. Flower pink. Leaf similar to Cox but not so dark. Grieve, 1858. F.C.C., R.H.S., 1872.

Medallion. Small flowers. Flower orange-red. Leaf pale green with cream and bronze patch in centre. U.S.A., 1960. '

Mr Henry Cox (Mrs Henry Cox). Dwarf, slow grower, single flower. Flower Begonia 619/2 shading to 619. Leaf, outer border Citron Green 763/3, shadow zone varying in intensity, Mandarin Red 17, irregular darker zone from Ivy Green 0001060/3 to black; inner colour Lavender Green 000761. Cannell, 1879. F.C.C., R.H.S., 1879. A.M., R.H.S. Trials, 1960, as Mrs Henry Cox.

Mrs Pollock. Single flower. Flower Dutch Vermilion 717/1. Leaf flat, dentate, outer border Citron Green 763, shadow zone Mandarin Red 17, with irregular dark zone ranging from Lavender Green 000761 to Ivy Green 0001060/3. Grieve, 1859. F.C.C., R.H.S., 1861.

(f) Miniature Group

(i) GREEN-LEAVED

Golden Harry Hieover. The largest variety in this section. Yellow-green foliage, chestnut zone; small vermilion flowers. Before 1880.

Grannie Hewitt. Very double scarlet flowers. Small green-zoned leaves.

Kleine Liebling (Hal, Petit Pierre, Little Darling). Perfect miniature. Single pink flower. Zoned light leaf. 1925.

Miriam Basey. Single, white flower, splashed red. Read, 1950.

(ii) BLACK-LEAVED

Claudius. Flower single, white marked Camellia Rose 622/1. Burrows, 1955.

Jenifer. Single large flower, Carmine 21. Parrett, 1962.

Nero. Very dwarf, large single flower. Flower Dutch Vermilion 717. Leaf as Claudius but with red flush and red stems. Burrows, 1955.

Opal. Very large, white flowers, edged purple. Parrett, 1960.

Orange Gnome. Single flowers. Flower orange. Leaf dark green. Parrett, 1959.

Pauline. Semi-double flower. Flower Carmine Rose 621/1, white reverse. Leaf dark green zoned. Parrett, 1962.

Red Black Vesuvius. Large single flowers, very dwarf. Flower Dutch Vermilion 717. Leaf Ivy Green 0001060/2. Cannell, 1890.

Salmon Black Vesuvius (Salmon Pixie). Single flower. Geranium Lake 20/3 shaded darker. Leaf as Red Black Vesuvius. Cannell, 1907.

Tiberius. Single flower, large. Flower Orient Red 819/3, shot Cherry 722. Leaf, very dark with black zone. Burrows, 1955.

Timothy Clifford. Small double flower. Flower, Porcelain Rose 620. Leaf as Claudius. Burrows, 1955.

Trajan. Large single flower. Flowers Signal Red 719, white eye. Leaf as Claudius. Burrows, 1955.

White Gem. Flower white. Parrett, 1958.

(iii) SILVER-LEAVED

Madame Butterfly. Double flower. Flower Currant Red. Leaf Olive Green butterfly on an ivory base. Thorpe, 1960.

Madame Salleron (Madame Salleroi, Dandy). Tufted habit, does not flower. Leaf green with irregular cream margin. Mathieu, Melun, 1877. Sport from Mangle's Variegated.

Silver Kewense. Very small grower. Flower Currant Red 821/2. Leaf green, edged white, occasionally tinged violet. Caledonian, 1956. Sport from Kewense.

Sprite. Single flower. Flower Salmon Coral. Leaf greyish-green with ivory border. Miller, U.S.A., 1949.

Variegated Kleine Liebling. Single flower. Flower Rhodamine Pink 29/1, upper petals based white. Leaf greyish-green with white border. Miller, U.S.A., 1956.

(iv) TRICOLOR

Elf. Single flower. Flower Scarlet. Leaf grey-green, wide yellow border flushed with scarlet. Miller, U.S.A., 1952.

75

Fairyland. Small single flower. Flower scarlet. Leaf, silver tricolor. Miller, U.S.A., 1951.

Nugget. Small single flower. Flower Phlox Pink. Leaf Olive Green with yellow border. Miller, U.S.A., 1955.

REGAL PELARGONIUMS

(*Pelargonium* × *domesticum* Bailey)

(5) Arranged according to principal colour impression of flower.

(i) WHITE

All My Love. Very large frilled flower, upper petals edged and splashed wine-red. Schmidt, U.S.A.

Annabel. Large flowers slightly frilled. Upper petals blotched with Lilac. Glass, 1950.

Bridesmaid. Large flowers. Magenta feathering on upper petals.

Bystock. Large flowers, blotched Maroon and Tyrian Purple.

Champion. Large ruffled flowers. Blotched Carmine.

Chilwell White. Large ruffled flowers. Slight crimson vein.

Doris Frith. Ruffled petals with veins of Fuchsine Pink. Ayton, 1953.

Duchess of Teck (Princess of Teck, Purity, Duchess). Sometimes lightly marked with rose. Cannell, 1900.

Edith. Lower petals white. Garnet, upper petals edged white.

Fondant. Spiraea Red veins on upper petals.

Gay Nineties. Large ruffled flowers. Tyrian Purple splashes. Schmidt, 1947.

Kantara. Small flowers. Garnet veins in upper petals.

Mrs R. G. Green (Magpie, Elsie). Small flowers, upper petals blotched Purple.

Muriel Harris. Large frilled flowers. Amethyst pencilling on upper petals. Ayton, 1953. F.C.C., R.H.S., 1958.

Pearl. Ruffled petals veined with Crimson.

Queen Hermione. Large flowers. Maroon splash on upper petals.

Royal Audrey. Large flowers, slightly marked with Purple.

Sunrise. Dark markings on upper petals.

The Doctor. Straggly grower, large flowers. Crimson feathering on upper petals.

Turtle's White. Unmarked.

Victoria Regina (Queen Bess). Ruffled petals, slight Purple blotch. Cannell, 1900.

Volonte Nationale. Rose markings in petals.
White Cloud. Large frilled flowers. Kerrigan, U.S.A., 1950.
White Swan. Large flowers, sometimes speckled with Carmine. Horner.

(ii) PINK

Admiral Beresford. Rose Red 724. Upper petals blotched maroon-white centre.

Albert Victor. China Rose 024/1. White edge to petals.

Alice Eastwood. Large flowers. Carmine Rose 621, with ruby-red splashes. Schmidt, U.S.A., 1948.

Angela. Rose Madder 23, white throat with darker blotches. Parrett, 1963.

Apple Blossom (Glorious). Pale Rose Madder with white centre. Cassidy, 1939.

Arabia. Large flowers. Neyron Rose 623, blotched purple and black.

Axminster. Very large flowers, semi-frilled, dusky pink-salmon, maroon blotch on upper petals. Circus Day seedling. Hickman, 1963.

Buckhurst (Vicar of Exmouth). Strong grower. Phlox Pink, crimson and maroon marks on upper petals.

Carisbrooke (Ballerina, Marechal Foch, Sunningdale Pink). Outstanding plant. Rhodamine Pink 527/2, upper petals feathered carmine. Hodges, 1928, A.M., R.H.S. Seedling of Queen Mary.

Carlotta. Rhodamine Pink 527/3, upper petals feathered crimson.

Carmine. Tyrian Rose 24/1 marked with Crimson and Maroon. Humphris, 1940. A.M., R.H.S.

Carole. Persian Rose 628, purple and black feathering.

Charmer. Large flowers. Pale Phlox Pink, upper petals shaded Dahlia Purple.

Cicely Tilden. Solferino Purple 26, scarlet shades, lighter throat, maroon marks.

Circus Day. Large flowers. Rose Opal 022, blotched Purple. Schmidt, U.S.A., 1951. A.M., R.H.S., 1961.

Comtesse de Choiseul (Sandringham). Amaranth Rose 530, crimson mark on all petals.

Delilah. Pale Tyrian Rose with maroon upper petals. U.S.A.

Devon Lass. Large ruffled flowers. Spiraea Red 025/2, purple marks on upper petals.

Dorothy. Neyron Rose 623, white edge. Hayes, 1900.

Edna Furby. Fuchsine Pink 267. Parrett, 1962.

Emmanuel Lias. White petals, heavily blotched pink. Balmont, 1900.

Ethelwyn Surtees. Small flowers, Geranium Lake, maroon blotches. Ayton, 1951.

Eunice. Amaranth Rose 520/3, upper petals blotched Carmine. Cole, 1956.

Exmouthian. Large flowers. Neyron Rose 623/2, upper petals heavily blotched.

Fascination (Royal Fascination). Large flowers. Pale Rose Madder, marked Turkey Red and Maroon on upper petals.

Gardener Divall. Large flowers. Phlox Pink 625, maroon and purple blotches in upper petals. Telston, 1952.

Gordon Newton Wells. Blushed Pink. Crimson and maroon marks on upper petals.

Grand Opera. Very large flowers. Pale pink, flushed crimson reverse. U.S.A.

Iona. Pale Carmine, white centre, scarlet and maroon upper petals.

Jean. Very large flowers. Amaranth Rose 530, heavily marked Tyrian Purple.

Keston Belle. Large flowers. Rose Madder 23/2, upper petals blotched purple and black.

Lady Edinburgh. Rose Bengal 25/2, upper petals blotched purple.

Lady Irene Burton. Camellia Rose and Indian Lake, maroon veins on upper petals. Telston, 1950.

Madame Thibaut. Frilled petals, white petals heavily marked Phlox Pink. Lemoine, 1900?

Maid of Devon. Very large flowers. Persian Rose 628, upper petals heavily blotched deeper.

Marilyn (Jack Bailey). Single flowers. Rhodamine Pink 527/2, Camellia Rose and maroon marks on upper petals. Telston, 1950. A reintroduction.

Mary Larkin. Fuchsine Pink 627, upper petals blotched darker. Parrett, 1958.

Melbourne. Large flowers. Rose Opal 022, blotched maroon. Cole, 1952.

Mrs A. Norris. Fuchsine Pink edged with white, blotched Tyrian Purple.

Mrs Innes Rogers (Sugar Plum). Crimson 22/1. White edges and white centre. Wisley Trials, 1951.

Mrs W. J. Godfrey. Neyron Rose 623/2. Upper petals feathered purple and red.

Mrs E. Hickman. Very large flower; a better version of Delilah. Hickman, 1963.

Muriel Hawkins. Large flowers. Soft pink. Ayton, 1960.

Our Francis. Large flowers. Rhodamine Pink 527/3, upper petals blotched purple-red.

List of Species and Varieties

Paso Robles. Large flower. Rhodamine Pink 527, shaded and blotched Rose Bengal and Cardinal Red. U.S.A., 1942.

Paul Lamerie. Roseine Purple, Fuchsia Purple and Garnet Lake markings on upper petals.

Princess of Wales. Nearly double frilled flower. Carmine 21, white centre and white edges to petals. The best regal of 1877.

Ray Kellog. Ruffled petals. Carmine Rose 621, blotched and veined darker. Jarrett, 1946.

Ray Storr. Large flowers. Rose Madder 23 with white centre. Telston. A renamed introduction.

Roseeka. Crimson 22/2, upper petals blotched purple and black.

Rose Martin. Large ruffled flower. Neyron Rose 623, lower petals lighter, white throat. Parrett, 1963.

Rose Slam. Rose Madder 23, dark blotches on upper petals, lower petals Rose Madder 23/1. Parrett, 1963.

Rosy Morn. Single flowers. Rose Madder 23, upper petals blotched maroon.

Royal Eve (Eva). Large flowers. Rose Madder 23.

Sienna. Large flowers. Rhodamine Pink 527/1, upper petals carmine and maroon.

Sue Jarrett. Large blooms. Phlox Pink 625/2, petals flushed Cherry Red. Jarrett, U.S.A., 1940.

Summertime. Small flowers. White, heavily blotched with Scarlet 19. U.S.A.

Talisman (Mrs V. G. Cooke). Neyron Rose 623/3. Upper petals edged Orient Red.

Violet Warneford. Large flowers. Tyrian Rose 24/1, white centres feathered maroon.

Vogue. Solferino Purple 26, lighter throat, Indian Lake veins. Telston, 1954.

William Pascoe. Crimson 22/2 white centre, upper petals blotched purple.

(iii) RED

Aubusson. Very large flower. Mrs Innes Rogers × Dazzler seedling. Hickman, 1962.

Bonnard. White base, bold Carmine Lake markings. Ayton, 1962.

Caprice. Large flowers. Tyrian Rose 24, slight blotching. Rober, 1946. English stocks came from Italy.

Charles E. Pearson. Small flowers. Orient Red 819, heavily marked maroon.

Cheriton. Cherry 722, lighter centre, upper petals marked with maroon. Telston, 1950.

79

Cherrystone. Crimson 22/1, feathered purple and black.
Chorus Girl. Deep rose shading to bluish-pink at centre.
Commander Peary. Solferino Purple 26, shaded red, upper petals veined purple.
Countess of Feversham. Carmine Rose flared maroon. Ayton, 1962.
Crimson Lake. Crimson 22, heavily blotched on all petals, black and purple. Telston, 1950.
Dazzler. Dwarf grower. Geranium Lake, maroon marks on upper petals.
Decorator (Royal Decorator). Geranium Lake, maroon splashes on upper petals, white throat. Hayes, 1890?
Duke of Brandenburg. Geranium Lake, maroon marks on upper petals.
Evelyn Cole. Large flowers. Carmine 21, blotched maroon. Cole.
Evening Star. Small flowers. Crimson 22 with white centre.
Feldmarschall Mackensen (Mackensen). Large flowers. Rose Madder 23/1, marked with purple and scarlet. Faiss. Germany.
Fire Dancer. Cherry 722/1, upper petals veined purple. U.S.A.
Foxtrot. Cherry Red and white, dark marks in centre.
Geoffrey Heard. Persian Rose 628 and Crimson 22.
Godetia. Frilled flower. Carmine with white markings.
Gorgon. Frilled petals. Crimson 22/1, upper petals blotched black and purple.
Grandeur (Douglas). Tall habit. Claret Rose 021, purple and black blotches on all petals.
Grand Slam. Large flowers. Cherry 722/3, boldly marked Dahlia Purple. Schmidt, U.S.A., 1950. A.M., R.H.S., 1956. F.C.C., 1961.
House and Garden. Carmine 21, top petals maroon, pale Rhodamine Pink centre. Telston, 1954. Named after the periodical.
James Vance. Carmine 21/1, upper petals marked black. Telston, 1952.
Joan Fontaine. Claret Rose 021, blotched and veined black. Jarrett, U.S.A., 1942. There is already a zonal pelargonium with the same name.
Kathleen. Carmine with crimson markings.
Lady Mary Davy. Tyrian Rose 24, blotched with purple on upper petals.
Lady Twysden (Lady Torsden, Lady Tursden, Lady Twisden, Lady Forsden). Cardinal Red, Persian Rose at the throat, upper petals shaded maroon.
Lord Mayor Treloar. Claret Rose 021, white centre, purple feathering in upper petals.

Marie Vogel (Pink Vogel, Carnival). Large flowers. Cherry 722/3, upper petals heavily marked dark red. Faiss, 1920? A.M., R.H.S., 1951, as Carnival.

Marquis of Carisbrooke. Large flowers. Petals Carmine Rose, upper petals feathered Currant Red. A.M., R.H.S., 1962.

Mrs Gordon Edward. Blood Red with darker marks.

Mrs Howell Powell. Large flowers. Pale Phlox Pink, crimson splashes on upper petals. Purple blotches.

Mrs Jessell. Currant Red, Rose Madder veins, maroon markings on upper petals.

Mrs R. Wooton. Rose Bengal 25, Blood Red and black markings on upper petals.

Nicholas. Geranium Lake 20, white throat, purple marks on upper petals.

Patricia Coates (Joy, Joyful). Large flowers. Crimson 22/1, blotched maroon.

Penelope (Talara). Fuchsine Pink, Rose Bengal, upper petals heavily marked with purple.

Polonaise. Orient Red with maroon markings.

Radiant. Rose Madder and Turkey Red, maroon marks on upper petals.

Ruby. Cherry Red 722/2, upper petals blotched purple. Cole.

Stephen Godfrey. Carmine with maroon marks on all petals.

Stoneleigh. Small flowers. Rose Bengal 25, upper petals blotched and veined. Ayton, 1956. Renamed.

Wolfgang Von Goethe. Small flowers. Spiraea Red 025, purple blotches. German, 1906.

(iv) SALMON

Dolores. Very large blooms, pale salmon, maroon feathering. U.S.A.

Harvest Moon. Salmon Apricot, maroon

Joan Fairman. Frilled flowers. Pale pink. Upper petals shaded maroon. Ayton, 1962.

Salmon Splendour. Large flowers. Porcelain Rose 620, veined and blotched purple. U.S.A., Kerrigan, 1942.

Salmon Springtime. Soft salmon, shading to peachy-pink.

Valencia. Large flowers. Porcelain Rose 620, upper petals marked maroon. Case, U.S.A., A.M., R.II.S., 1963.

(v) ORANGE

Degas. Orange Red shading to crimson. Ayton, 1962.

Edward Perkins. Signal Red 719, flushed Rose Bengal, upper petals blotched maroon.

Elena Bennett. Rose Pink shaded to Carmine Pink, overlaid with cream.
Enid Blackaby. Crimson Orange overlaid Tile Red. A.M., R.H.S., 1960.
Fanny Eden. Scarlet 19/1, white throat, upper petals veined purple.
Grossmama Fischer (Grandma Fisher). Dwarf grower, frilled petals, Orange Pink with dark splashes. Faiss.
Kardomah. Very large flower, orange-red upper petals, blotched purple and silver. Hickman, 1963.
J. A. Murdocke. Compact plant. Orange Red.
Orange Prince. Geranium Lake 20/1.
Orange Sal. Rose Opal 022/1, shading to coral, slightly blotched purple. U.S.A.
Persimmon. Signal Red 719/2. Upper petals blotched dark maroon. F.C.C., R.H.S., 1897.
Senorita. Cherry 722/2. Lighter centre, upper petals blotched Dahlia Purple. Cassidy, U.S.A.
Solano. Large flowers. Empire Rose 0621. Maroon blotches on all petals. Howard, U.S.A.
Washington. Light Orange Red, maroon marks in the centre.
Weston Dazzler. Geranium Lake 20, upper petals veined purple and crimson.

(vi) MAGENTA

Alice West. Compact plant. Mauve 633/1, maroon blotches. Parrett, 1962.
Anne Milham. Rhodamine Purple 29/1, darker marks on upper petals, edged white. Parrett, 1962.
Atlante. Very large flowers. Petunia Purple 32/2, blotched darker on upper petals, white centre.
Baroness Swanborough. Orchid Purple, maroon marks.
Blush Queen. Large flowers. Petunia Purple 32/3, large blotches on upper petals.
Blytheswood (Duchess of Cornwall). Purple Rose, magenta markings, white edge.
Chelsea. Large flowers. Orchid Purple 31/2, blotched darker on all petals.
Chicago Market. Large flowers. Persian Rose 628/3.
Connie Edmunds. Rose Purple 533, darker purple markings on all petals. Telston, 1950.
Console. Lavender, upper petals marked with mahogany. Parrett, 1960.
Diadem. Pale Mallow Purple, upper petals Violet Purple. Telston, 1950.
Edith. Large flowers. Garnet Lake and Phlox Pink.

Ella. Very large flowers. Cyclamen Purple, upper petals heavily blotched darker.

Favourite. Phlox Purple with petunia veins.

Florrie Griggs. Orchid Purple 31/2, all petals blotched crimson and purple.

Fred W. Fletcher. Mauve 33/2, upper petals marked purple and crimson.

Geoffrey Horsman. Mauve 633, blotched deep purple. Telston, 1952.

Hamlet et Ophelie (Patricia). Shades of mauve with purple blotches on upper petals.

Helen Ludgate. Very large flowers. Paeony Purple, upper petals marked maroon. Telston, 1950.

Hester Bateman. Tyrian Rose 24, heavily blotched Dahlia Purple, especially on upper petals. Telston, 1950.

Hilda Jefford. Large flowers. Mallow Purple 630, upper petals marked crimson. Telston, 1952. A sport of Carnival.

Ivo Mitchell. Soft pinkish lavender, upper petals feathered with purple.

Jane Shaw. Deep mauve.

Jean Fielding. Cyclamen Purple 30/2. Upper petals blotched deep purple. Ayton, 1955. A Helen Ludgate seedling.

Joan Chandler. Phlox Purple 623/1. Maroon blotches on upper petals, white throat. Parrett, 1962.

King Haakon (Dr Masters). Pale Beetroot Purple, purple markings on all petals.

Lavender Grand Slam. Silvery-mauve. Sport of Grand Slam. A.M., R.H.S., 1962. F.C.C., 1963.

Lilac Domino. Very large flowers. Mauve 633/3, upper petals blotched Cyclamen Purple. Telston, 1950. A Carisbrooke seedling.

Marie Rober. Very large flowers. Garnet Lake 828/3, all petals blotched with Dahlia Purple. U.S.A.

Modigliani. Orchid Mauve, overlaid with violet. Ayton, 1961.

Mrs Egbert Anderson (Tatge). Solferino Purple, darker markings.

Mrs Langtry. Dwarf grower, small plant. Petunia Purple 22, marked Dahlia Purple on upper petals, white throat.

Nancy, Lady Astor. Ruffled flowers. Mauve, shading to lavender.

Neuheit Carl Faiss. Mauve 633/2, all petals marked Dahlia Purple. Faiss.

Parisiana. Mauve 633/1, Dahlia Purple marks on upper petals. Renamed 1954.

Paul Storr. Tyrian Rose 24, blotched with purple on all petals. Telston, 1950.

83

Persia. Very large flower, veined and splashed with purple. Mrs Langtry × Rhodamine.

Quakeress (San Diego). Roseine Purple 629, heavily blotched Dahlia Purple and crimson. Germany.

Queen Mary. Large flowers. Mallow Purple, upper petals blotched deeper.

Rhoda. Phlox Purple 632/1, dark blotches on upper petals. Parrett, 1960.

Rhodamine. Very large flowers. Phlox Purple, maroon marks on upper petals, white centre. Telston, 1950. Helen Ludgate × Mrs Langtry.

Rose of Devon. Persian Rose 628/1.

Ruby Twysden (Mary Glen, Ruby Tursden). Rhodamine Purple, paler at the centre. Telston, 1950. Sport from Lady Twysden.

Stardust. Large flowers. Pale lavender, flushed rosy-violet. U.S.A.

Telston's Prima. Amaranth Rose with maroon marks.

Violet Regina (Regina). White with heavy Dahlia Purple and Turkey Red splashes on all petals.

Violetta. Violet-blue.

Waltztime. Large ruffled petals. Phlox Purple 632/2, upper petals blotched red and purple. Schmidt, U.S.A., 1942.

(vii) BLACK

Black Butterfly (Brown's Butterfly). Short, compact grower. Velvety-black flowers, flecked mahogany-red. Brown, U.S.A., 1953.

Black Knight (Black Prince, Pansy). Dahlia Purple 931, edged white.

Burgundy. Ruffled petals. Cardinal Red and Indian Lake overlaid with velvet black. Brown, U.S.A., 1946.

Conspicuous. Wine red, lower petals edged with black. Brown, U.S.A., 1947.

Dusky Maid. Tyrian Purple, overlaid with black.

Jungle Night. Very large flowers. Indian Lake 826, blotched black. Brown, U.S.A., 1946.

Lord Bute (Purple Robe). Small flowers, dark maroon with narrow Fuchsia Purple edge. A.M., R.H.S., 1910.

Lynne Fontaine. Black Maroon, shading to red and violet.

Manx Maid. Dwarf grower. Chocolate Maroon.

Marchioness of Bute. Small frilled flowers. Maroon 10/30, centre lighter, distinct edge of Rose Madder 23.

Prince John (Nubian). Small flowers. Very dark red and maroon, upper petals almost covered with black.

Red Velvet. Large flower. Garnet Lake 828, large black marks. Brown, U.S.A., 1945.

Rhapsody. Large flowers. Crimson Black, all petals blotched with black. Kerringham, U.S.A., 1942.

Shiraz. Large flower; compact grower; dark magenta, white eye. Hickman, 1963.

Virtue. Compact plant. Deep Mahogany Red, white throat, large black blotches. Parrett, 1960.

Windward Jane. Very small flower. Rhodamine Purple 29/1, heavily blotched with black.

Zulu King. Crimson 22, upper petals heavily marked black. Brown, 1947.

IVY-LEAVED PELARGONIUMS

(a) **Single-flowered,** of which the flowers have normally five petals.

Butterflies. Large flowers. Cyclamen Purple 30/1. Schmidt, U.S.A., 1948.

Château de Cadmine. Zoneless leaf. Carmine flower with paler marks on upper petals.

Florive. Large flowers. Light Purple Pink.

Jeanne d'Arc. Dwarf habit, thin flowers. Whitish-mauve, veined carmine. Lemoine, 1880.

L'Elégante. Dwarf habit, leaves small: white edges which show mauve tints. Flower: white flushed Magenta 273, with some crimson feathering. Cannell, 1868. F.C.C., R.H.S., 1872.

Madame Margot. Variegated leaf. Rose-pink flower.

Mrs Hawley. Large flowers. Crimson with darker marks on upper petals

Sir A. Hort. Pale Rose Madder with darker markings

Vicar of Shirley. Vigorous grower. Geranium Lake. Cannell, 1910.

(b) **Double-flowered,** of which the form is fundamentally that of the single-flowered but the petals normally exceed five.

Abel Carrière. Tyrian Purple 727/3. Cannell, 1884.

Alice Crousse (Nymphaea). Large flowers. Orchid Purple 31. Bruant, 1890.

Beauty of Castlehill. Rose Pink. A.M., R.H.S., 1891.

Beauty of Jersey. Reddish-purple. Bealby, 1895.

Carnival (Fanfaronnade). Large flowers. Roseine Purple 629/2, blotched on all petals with rose-red. Schmidt, U.S.A., 1942. Sport from Leopard.

Pelargoniums for all Purposes

Colonel Baden Powell (Lord Baden Powell). Very large flowers. White, shaded Magenta 273, upper petals blotched Tyrian Purple 727. Lemoine, 1900.

Comtesse de Grey. Large flower. Magenta 27.

Dr Chipault. Solferino Purple.

Duchesse de Valentinois (The Duchess). Large, thin flowers. White marked with Tyrian Purple. Schmidt, U.S.A., 1948, as The Duchess.

Eclipse. Pale Rose Madder.

El Gaucho. Fuchsia Purple 28/1. Schmidt, 1945.

General Championette. Signal Red 719/3. Bruant, 1890.

Gladiator. Rose-red.

H.M. The King. Large flowers. Deep Salmon Pink. Cannell, 1900.

H.M. The Queen. Salmon Pink. Cannell, 1900.

Horne's Achievement. Crimson Orange, darker markings on upper petals.

Jester. Orchid Purple 31/2, all petals striped and blotched Solferino Purple. Schmidt, U.S.A., 1942.

King Edward VII. Large flowers. Rose Red 724/1, upper petals feathered darker.

La France. Large flowers. Phlox Purple 632/1, with darker markings. Cannell, 1900.

Leopard. Large flowers. Lilac Pink, blotched crimson. Cannell, 1900.

L'Etincelant (Scarlet Crousse). Turkey Red. Sport of Madame Crousse.

Louis Thibaut. Pale Tyrian Purple.

Lucky Strike. Tyrian Rose 24, upper petals marked Tyrian Purple. Schmidt, U.S.A., 1946.

Madame Crousse (Emily Sylvia). Large flowers, Solferino Purple 26/2. Cannell, 1900.

Madame Lauthier. Rose Madder, shaded crimson.

Mauve Queen. Pale mauve, Orchid Purple veins.

Mrs Perrin. Dwarf habit, Rose Purple 533.

Neon. Large flowers. Fuchsia Purple. Schmidt, U.S.A., 1942.

Olivia. Pink, with petals flaked white. Hickman. 1964.

Orchard Blossom. White, with magenta veins. U.S.A.

Rose Crousse. Pale Rose Madder.

Sir Percy Blakeney. Large flowers, Geranium Lake 20. Wright 1920. A.M., R.H.S., 1923.

Snowdrift. Strong grower. White, 1963.

The Bride (Bridesmaid). Large flowers. Mallow Purple 630/2, upper petals marked Tyrian Purple. Schmidt, U.S.A., 1942.

Trophee. Rose Bengal.

List of Species and Varieties

(c) **Rosette,** having smaller flowers with petals exceeding five, more or less equal in size, and altering the shape of the flower.

Beatrice Cottington. Rather dwarf habit. Persian Rose 628. Cottington, 1951.

Beauty of Eastbourne. Tyrian Purple shot with Persian Rose. Cannell, 1910.

Blue Peter (Eulalia). Dwarf grower. Phlox Purple 621/1, darker blotches. Cannell, 1910.

Eastbourne Beauty. Strong grower. Pale rose-red flowers. Cottington, 1951.

Galilee. Very good bedder. Persian Rose 628/1. Lemoine.

Lilac Gem. Dwarf plant. Dark small leaves. Bishops Violet 24/3.

Madame Cachin. Dwarf habit. Blush white.

Madame Rozaine. Dwarf habit. Mauve-pink. Rozaine.

Mrs W. A. R. Clifton. Large flowers. Orient Red 819. Clifton, 1920.

Mrs W. H. Martin. Dwarf grower. Petunia Purple 32/3. Bruant, 1908.

Red Galilee. Compact plant. Bright scarlet. Sport from Galilee.

Ryecroft Surprise. Fuchsine Pink 627. Jones of Lewisham. A.M., R.H.S., 1895.

Souvenir de Charles Turner. Persian Rose 628. Lemoine.

Tiberias. Dwarf grower. Solferino Purple.

Willy (Berkeley Red, Incomparable). Very large flowers, strong grower Turkey Red 721. Lemoine, 1900.

HYBRID IVY-LEAVED PELARGONIUMS

Achievement. Semi-double flower. Rose Madder 23/1, veined pink. Cannell, 1900.

James T. Harrison. Semi-double. Orient Red 819. A.M., 1908.

Milky Way. Dwarf habit, semi-double flowers. White. Miller, U.S.A., 1946.

Millfield Gem (Lady Brooke). Semi-double flower. Fuchsia Purple 28/3, blotched darker. Lemoine, 1894.

Mrs Hamilton. Semi-double flowers. Signal Red 219/2, flushed orange.

Mrs John Day. Semi-double flowers. Crimson. A.M., 1900.

SCENTED-LEAVED PELARGONIUMS

Attar of Roses (Otto of Roses of Andrews). Dwarf habit. Leaves pinnate. Flower Lavender. Scent rose. Cannell, 1900.

Clorinda. Leaves large trilobed. Strong grower. Flowers: Solferino Purple 26/2, upper petals streaked pink and purple. Scent eucalyptus. Cannell, 1907. A.M., R.H.S.

Crispum Minus (Fingerbowl Geranium). Leaves very small. Flower single, pale Mauve. Scent citron.

Endsleigh. Leaves denticulate, 5-lobed. Flower Lavender. Scent sharp pepper. Illustrated by Andrews.

Fair Ellen (Fair Helen). Dwarf habit. Leaves dark green, shaped like an oak-leaf, sticky. Flowers Lavender. Scent pungent.

Filicifolium (Fernaefolium). Leaves fern-like. Flower Orchid Purple. Scent balsam.

Fragrans. Leaves small, reniform. Flower white. Scent pine. 1800. A primary hybrid.

Joy Lucille. Leaves pinnate, grey-green, felted. Scent peppermint. U.S.A., 1940.

Lady Mary. Leaves pale green. Flower Magenta blotched Solferino Purple. Scent nutmeg. Before 1800.

Lady Plymouth. Dwarf habit. Leaves pinnate, grey-green edged with cream. Flower Phlox Pink 625/3. Scent rose. Before 1800.

Lady Scarborough. Leaves very small. Flowers Amaranth Rose. Scent lemon. 1774. This may be *P. hermanniifolium*.

Little Gem (Terebinthinaceum). Similar to Attar of Roses. Scent pungent.

Pretty Polly. Dwarf habit. Leaves dentate. Scent almond.

Prince of Orange. Leaves small. Flowers pale Mauve. Scent orange. Before 1880.

Queen of Lemons. Leaves crenate. Flower Violet. Scent strong lemon. Before 1800.

Variegated Crispum (Variegated Prince Rupert). Leaves cream and green, crenate. Flower Lavender, carmine veined. Scent lemon. Before 1868.

UNIQUE PELARGONIUMS

Claret Rock. Leaves deeply lobed. Flowers Tyrian Rose 24, upper petals marked purple.

Colville's Storksbill (Scarlet Unique). Flower Signal Red 719/3, upper petals marked maroon. Colville, 1819.

Crimson Unique. Flowers Spinel Red and Turkey Red, all petals marked and veined black. Before 1880.

Jessel's Unique. Flowers Neyron Rose 623, upper petals veined purple. Caledonian, 1953. A re-introduction.

Madame Nonin. Flowers Neyron Rose 623, shaded and veined Turkey Red. Nonin, 1870. This could be Monsieur Ninon, an old Belgian variety.

Mrs Kingsbury. Leaves dentate, dark green. Flower Tyrian Rose, marked with purple. Before 1880.

Paton's Unique. Similar to Madame Nonin, but smaller. Paton, 1870.

Pink Pet. Dwarf habit, small flowers. Camellia Rose 622, upper petals marked dark red. Caledonian, 1953. Sport of Scarlet Pet.

Purple Unique. Flowers pale Petunia Purple, darker purple marks on upper petals.

Rollinson's Unique. Flowers Tyrian Purple, veined darker. Rollison, before 1880.

Rose Unique (Pink Unique). Flowers Neyron Rose, veined darker.

Scarlet Pet (Moore's Victory). Dwarf habit, small flowers. Turkey Red 721/2, upper petals Indian Lake and Crimson.

Select Storksbill. Large grower, large flowers. Neyron Rose 623/1, upper petals marked and veined black. 1819.

Shrubland Pet. Dwarf grower, small flowers. Neyron Rose 623, red and purple shading on upper petals.

Unique Aurore. Flowers large, Orient Red 819/1, feathered maroon, lower petals nearly black.

White Unique. Strong grower. Flowers white, tinted Roseine Purple.

ANGEL PELARGONIUMS

Catford Belle. Roseine Purple, upper petals marked Dianthus Purple. Langley-Smith, 1935.

Chinese Coral. White, Dianthus Purple marks on upper petals. Langley-Smith.

Kerlander. Mallow Purple 630, Cyclamen Purple 30 on upper petals. Langley-Smith, 1940.

Mrs Dumbrill. Mauve 633/2, marked with Orchid Purple. Langley-Smith, 1940.

Mrs H. G. Smith. Pale Salmon Pink with rose markings. Langley-Smith.

Rose Bengal. Rose Purple 533/3, upper petals Dianthus Purple, pale edges to petals. Langley-Smith, 1940.

Sancho Panza. Larger than usual in this section. Dahlia Purple, paling to Cyclamen Purple at edges. Telston.

Shirley Ash. Pale mauve with Cyclamen marks on upper petals. Langley-Smith.

Solferino. Pale Mallow Purple, purple marks on upper petals. Langley-Smith.

SPECIES

The following is but a small selection of the *Pelargonium* species, but it does include those commonly found in nurserymen's lists.

P. abrotanifolium. Thin, straggly growth. Leaves small, much divided. Flowers single, white, veined purple. Scent southernwood. Introduced from South Africa, 1796.

P. acetosum. Slender stems. Leaves silvery-green. Flowers single, shades of Porcelain Rose. Introduced 1794. Cape.

P. angulosum. Very hairy plant. Leaves truncate, toothed lobes. Flowers single, purple with maroon veins on upper petals. Introduced 1724, from the Cape.

P. cucullatum. Tall, shrubby plant. Flowers large, Doge Purple with darker veins. 1687. Ancestor of the regals. Found commonly near Cape Town.

P. denticulatum. Leaves deeply cut, flat. Flowers Amaranth Rose. Scent balsam. Introduced 1789.

P. echinatum (The Sweetheart Geranium). Leaves glaucous, spiny stems, deciduous, tuberous. Flowers small, white, pink or purple, upper petals blotched magenta. 1794, Namaqualand. Miss Stapleton and *echinatum* Album are only colour variations of this.

P. gibbosum (The Gouty Geranium). Tall, shrubby succulent plant, swollen joints on stems. Leaves glaucous. Flowers very small, Barium Yellow 503/1. Flowers scented after dusk. 1712.

P. graveolens (The Rose-scented Geranium). Shrubby plant. Leaves deeply lobed. Flowers small, pink, marked with purple. Introduced 1774; the parent of many rose-scented varieties.

P. inquinans. Flowers single, Dutch Vermilion 717. Introduced 1714 by Bishop Compton. This is an ancestor of the zonals.

P. multibracteatum. Straggly habit. Leaves deeply lobed, zoned dark green. Flowers single, white, small, purple flush at throat. Introduced 1892, from Abyssinia.

P. odoratissimum (The Apple-scented Pelargonium). Dwarf plant. Leaves light green, velvety. Flowers very small, white. Scent apple. Introduced 1724 from South Africa.

P. peltatum. Trailing habit. Leaves bright green, fleshy. Flowers single, pale mauve. Introduced 1701. One of the parents of the ivy-leaved geraniums.

P. quercifolium (Nelson). Short-jointed plant. Leaves oak-leaf shape. Flowers single, mauve, marked darker. Scent pungent. Introduced 1774. From South Africa.

P. radens (*P. radula*). Leaves rough with narrow straight lobes. Flowers pink, marked with purple. Scent strong rose. Introduced 1774. From South Africa.

P. saxifragoides. Very dwarf ivy-leaved type. Leaves very dark green and fleshy. Flowers very small, mauve with Cyclamen Purple marks. Introduced 1888 from South Africa.

P. scandens. Large straggly plant. Leaves zoned. Flowers pale rose. Similar to *P. acetosum*. Introduced 1792.

P. stenopetalum. Slender plant. Leaves dentate. Flowers single, coral red. Introduced 1710 from South Africa.

P. tetragonum. Tall, straggly plant. Small bright green leaves. Stems succulent, four-sided. Flowers small, single, white, with maroon stamens. Introduced 1774.

P. tomentosum. Bushy, spreading plant. Leaves soft, flannelly, grey-green. Flowers very small, white. Scent strong peppermint. 1790.

P. tricolor (*P. violarium*). Shrubby, branching growth. Leaves sage green. Flowers single, upper petals magenta, black spots at base, lower petals white. 1792 from South Africa.

P. triste (The Sad Geranium). Tuberous variety. Long carrot-like leaves. Flowers small, brownish with yellow margins. Sweet scented after dusk. 1632 by Tradescant. Possibly the first geranium to be introduced into England from the Cape.

P. zonale. Tall, half-shrub. Leaves faintly zoned. Flowers single, either white, pink, red or purple. Very common in South Africa. Introduced 1700.

INDEX OF VARIETIES AND SPECIES

VARIETIES

93

Catford Belle, 22, 89
Champion, 76
Charentin, 66
Charles Blair, 59
Charles E. Pearson, 79
Charles Gounoud, 69
Charmer, 77
Château de Cadmine, 85
Chavarri Hermanos, 66
Chelsea, 82
Chelsea Gem, 71
Cherison, 66
Cheriton, 79
Cherrystone, 80
Chicago Market, 82
Chilwell White, 76
Chinese Coral, 89
Chinese Dragon, 71
Chorus Girl, 80
Cicely Tilden, 77
Circus Day, 77
Clarence Elliot, 61
Claret Rock, 88
Claudius, 47, 75
Cleopatra, 58
Clere Pink, 58
Clorinda, 21, 88
Cloth of Gold, 72
Colonel Baden Powell, 86
Colonel Drabbe, 66
Colville's Storksbill, 88
Commander Peary, 80
Comtesse de Grey, 86
Comtesse de Choiseul, 77
Connie Edmunds, 82
Console, 82
Conspicuous, 84
Constance, 58
Copper Kettle, 59
Corallina, 70
Coronation, 58
Coronia, 70
Countess of Faversham, 80
Countess of Jersey, 34, 58
Crampel's Master, 73
Creed's Seedling, 72
Crimson Lake, 80
Crimson Unique, 22, 88
Crispum Minus, 88
Crispum Variegatum, 21, 33, 56
Crystal Palace Gem, 73
C. W. Ward, 58

Cymric, 59

Dagata, 56, 65
Darenth, 59
David Blake, 59
Dazzler, 80
Decorator, 33, 66, 80
Deep Skelly's, 61
Degas, 81
Delicata, 65
Delight, 58
Delilah, 77
Devon Lass, 77
Diadem, 82
Distinction, 19, 73
Dodd's Super Double, 55, 66
Dolly Varden, 72
Dolores, 81
Doris Frith, 76
Doris Moore, 25, 47, 59
Dorothy, 77
Dorothy Navarro, 57
Double Jacoby, 67
Double New Life, 69
Double Pink Bird's Egg, 69
Dr Chipault, 86
Dr M. Tyrs, 68
Drummer Boy, 60
Dryden, 34, 55, 60
Duchess, 65
Duchess of Teck, 76
Duchesse de Valentinois, 86
Duke of Brandenburg, 80
Dusky Maid, 84
Dutch Double Scarlet, 67

Eastbourne Beauty, 87
Eclipse, 86
Ecstasy, 63
Edelweiss, 64
Eden Beauty, 60
Eden Perfection, 58
Eden Roc, 60
Edith, 76, 82
Edmund Lachenal, 67
Edna Furby, 77
Edward Hockey, 34, 61
Edward Perkins, 81
E. Herbert, 69
Electric Pink, 67
Elena Bennett, 82
Elf, 75

Index of Varieties and Species

95

G

Index of Varieties and Species

SPECIES

GENERAL INDEX

General Index